Unstoppable Women

Owning Our Voices and Leading Change

Cathy Holt

Want to fully step into your leadership potential and get the most out of this book?

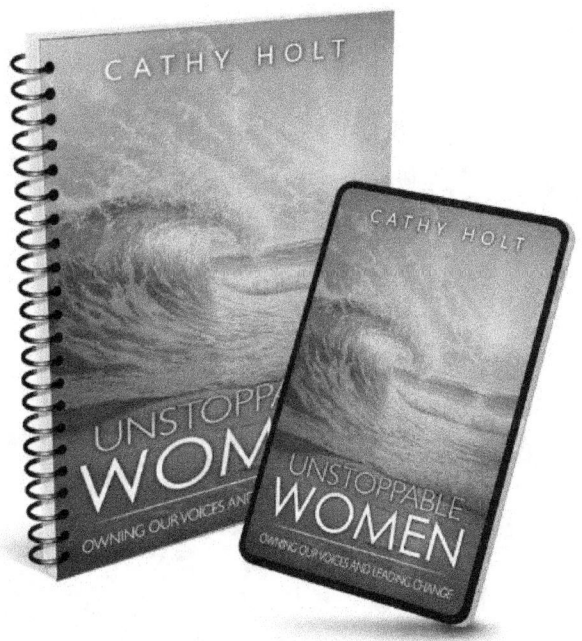

I'd like to gift you a downloadable companion Workbook so you can jot down your thoughts, note the areas that stand out to you, and answer the prompts at the end of each chapter, which will guide you in owning *your* voice.

Download this gift at:
www.cathyholt.com/unstoppableworkbook

Or with this QR Code:

Acknowledgments

Writing *Unstoppable Women: Owning Our Voices, Leading Change* has been a heartfelt journey of commitment to my passion of creating a movement of women leaders. Now, more than ever, we need their compassionate leadership that is human-centered and promotes collaboration over cutthroat competition.

To my daughter**, Laura Toledo**, whose courage, spirit, and tenacity in confronting the challenges she has faced as a teenage stroke survivor inspired me to live in the "evolution zone"—the space where I had to challenge my limiting beliefs, discover new strengths, and define and create the life I truly want...

Watching you thrive in the face of challenges has been a constant reminder of the strength we carry within us. Your perseverance, determination, and unwavering spirit have shown me what it truly means to be unstoppable. You have taught me that leadership is not just about standing tall but about rising again and again, no matter the obstacles. Thank you for being my light, my heart, and my greatest teacher.

To **Deb Drummond**, another unstoppable woman, who welcomed me into your world of *Show Up Stand Up Speak Up, Yes You!*—thank you for your boundless energy, creativity, and wisdom that inspired me to see new possibilities and step more boldly into my own power. Your generosity, insights, and unwavering belief in what's possible have expanded my impact in ways I never imagined. I am deeply grateful for the doors you've helped open and the heights you've encouraged me to reach. Your passion and drive are contagious, and I am forever grateful for the way you have challenged, supported, and championed me on this journey

To my sister, Becky, and my nephew, Holt—thank you for your encouragement and for reminding me to find humor even when frustration over gender inequities threatened to consume me.

Your laughter, perspective, and ability to lighten the moment kept me grounded and moving forward. I'm so grateful for you both.

I would like to acknowledge the unstoppable Sarah Oliveira, whose dynamic, energizing personality brought a vibrant energy to our home during her time as an exchange student. As my other "Brazilian" daughter, she has remained true to her passion for advancing Brazilian music, and her dedication continues to inspire those around her.

I have been so fortunate to have so many women guide and inspire me throughout my life. Through *Unstoppable Women* I want to honor the inspiring and resilient women who have allowed me into their lives. Thank you all for lifting up your voices and sharing your wisdom.

Contents

Introduction

What would it be like to lead your own life?

As women, we've been conditioned to "go along to get along." How many times have you heard phrases like:

"Don't make waves."

"Don't be so bossy."

"Why are you being so emotional?"

"Your job is to take care of others."

"Good girls don't behave like that."

Sometimes, the messages are subtler, but they are woven into our daily experiences. We're told not to take up too much space, to put others' needs ahead of our own, to stay quiet, or to shrink into the background. Think about it: Have you ever let someone cut in line because speaking up might cause a scene? Or heard an offensive comment but stayed silent because you didn't want to seem confrontational or be labeled difficult? If you did speak up, did you begin with, "I'm sorry, but…"—as if apologizing for standing up for yourself or having boundaries?

But what does speaking up have to do with leadership? Everything.

Choosing to lead your life means rejecting those outdated expectations and stepping fully into your power. It's about finding the courage to balance strength with empathy and to break barriers while nurturing connections. Leading your life means filling your own cup first, reflecting on what you value, identifying your passions, and setting boundaries to live authentically in all areas of your life.

Choosing to step into leadership is a bold and empowering decision that can transform both your life and the lives of those around you. Leadership provides a chance to make a meaningful difference by driving change, shaping inclusive spaces, and advancing causes that matter deeply to you. It's a journey of discovering and embracing your unique strengths, growing your confidence, and developing the resilience needed to face challenges head-on. Becoming a leader also means creating opportunities—not only for yourself but for others, as you inspire, support, and mentor those who will follow in your footsteps. For women, leadership is more than a role; it's a powerful way to contribute, connect, and create a lasting impact in the world.

Leadership begins when you find the courage to use your voice. It comes from having confidence, self-awareness, and the ability to advocate for yourself and others. These are leadership qualities, and they begin from within. Leadership is not reserved for boardrooms or political offices—it's woven into the decisions you make and the actions you take every day. When you show up as your true self, your confidence grows, and so does your ability to inspire and influence others. Whether you are an aspiring leader or find yourself in a situation that requires you to lead, discovering your leadership superpowers will change your life.

Leadership in Action

I remember a defining moment from my childhood. My family had just moved to a rural, close-knit community, and I started at a small school where two grades shared each classroom. One day, I stepped into the hall and saw a teacher holding a chair, poised as if to strike someone. I froze, horrified until I realized the target of her threat was my little sister. We shared the close bond of being the new kids, and stuck together no matter what.

Despite it being one of the scariest moments in my young life, I yelled, "Don't you dare hurt my sister! I'm telling my parents!" I'd been raised to respect authority, and confronting a teacher felt unthinkable. But I couldn't stay silent. My heart pounded as the teacher turned her fury on me, but the commotion drew others into the hall, and the situation diffused.

The next day, I was afraid to go back to school, fearing I'd be ridiculed or punished for speaking out. But to my surprise, I was met with admiration. Older students praised me for my courage. I hadn't set out to be a leader—I simply acted to protect my sister—but that moment changed how others saw me and how I saw myself. At the time, I had no idea that what I was experiencing was leadership. But later, I realized that leadership sometimes means stepping into discomfort for what's right, even when it's terrifying.

The Evolution Zone

Let's be honest: stepping into leadership—whether in that classroom, a workplace, or a personal relationship—can feel like venturing far outside your comfort zone. It's scary, but also transformative. And, this discomfort is also where growth happens, where you step into your "evolution zone."

Here, you challenge the beliefs that hold you back, discover new strengths, gain the courage to let go of what no longer serves you and create space for the life you truly want. The initial discomfort fades, replaced by a sense of empowerment as you learn new skills, navigate challenges, and stand firm in your values.

Overcoming the Saboteur

Even as you grow, the inner critic—what some call imposter syndrome—may whisper doubts:

"I don't have the right skills."

"I'm not qualified."

"I don't have the experience."

"What if I fail?"

Our brain creates thoughts from past experiences, feelings, and knowledge. But negative thoughts can be changed. And you can't let them limit you. Remember: you are the expert of your own life. Your lived experiences, challenges, and triumphs have given you a unique perspective and voice, both of which are invaluable. Leadership doesn't come from a title or degree; it's built on authenticity, courage, and the willingness to use your voice to drive change. It's an ability to unify people around a common goal. Sharing your story and passion can inspire others to believe in possibilities.

Yes, stepping into leadership may bring scrutiny or challenges in unsupportive environments. But it also offers the opportunity to drive change, empower others, impact your personal life, and leave a legacy that reflects your values and passions.

For more than 35 years, I have worked energetically for gender equality and center-staging women in leadership and decision-making roles. I am an elite international speaker and author promoting women as change agents. I have mentored grassroots and community-based women and aspiring leaders throughout the globe to awaken their inner leader, speak their truth and transform themselves and their communities. Whether I am speaking at UN meetings, teaching courses on women and gender studies, advocating for women's issues in the political arena, or connecting with women, I passionately share my experiences, skills, and strategies of navigating the challenges of leading as women.

Leadership isn't always planned. Sometimes, it begins with an act of bravery or necessity. It isn't about perfection or having all the answers. It's about authenticity, courage, and the willingness to step up—even when it's uncomfortable. It's about creating a life that aligns with your values and passions, uplifting others along the way, and leaving a legacy that reflects your true self.

In this book, we'll explore how to awaken your inner leader and step into your power. You'll reflect on what matters most to you, assess your strengths, and learn to navigate challenges with confidence and resilience. I will share the stories of women who stepped into leadership not because they sought it, but because necessity called them to act or they saw something they couldn't ignore—a wrong to right, a gap to fill, or a vision for change that demanded their courage and commitment. I hope you will see yourself in their stories, relate in some way to their challenges, and come to recognize your own potential to blaze new trails.

Whether you see yourself as a leader or not, I promise you this: you already have what it takes to be a change agent.

Potential is just unharnessed power. So, unleash your potential and step into your power.

Your journey begins now. Are you ready to lead your life?

Chapter 1

Embracing the Power Within: Why Women Make Exceptional Leaders

Leadership is not a title of position. the ability to inspire and influence others to achieve a common goal. Gone are the days of the curmudgeon sitting in his office and barking out orders. That traditional way of leading depended on control and commands. The new paradigm of leadership doesn't just focus on results, but strives to create spaces where everyone can grow and succeed, no matter who they are or where they come from. It requires a strong sense of self-awareness, empathy, and understanding of how someone relates to and affects others. And... women are good at this!

Leadership is not defined by a single attribute, but by a constellation of traits and skills that create the ability to inspire, guide, and impact others positively. Many of these attributes used to be considered "soft skills." The world is finally catching on that having these sensitivities, now renamed interpersonal skills, makes for great leaders! Women possess a unique combination of these qualities that make them exceptional leaders. Often shaped by their experiences, responsibilities, and challenges, these traits enable women to lead with purpose, authenticity, and resilience.

In today's rapidly changing world, empowering women in leadership roles has become crucial for a diverse and inclusive society. You have what it takes to inspire others. By awakening the leader within you, you can make a positive impact and create a lasting legacy.

This chapter explores the inherent and cultivated qualities that empower women to step into their power and excel in leadership roles. Consider this a smorgasbord or tasting of traits that today's experts have identified as crucial to great leadership. I will go into more detail in subsequent chapters.

If you go through historic tomes on leadership, many of these are not even mentioned and when they are, they are soft skills. The traditional leadership model centered on "control, corrective action, individualistic decision-making" according to a report by the consulting firm McKinsey.

But in 2019, LinkedIn conducted a global survey that asked hiring professionals how important these interpersonal skills were in hiring. Of the respondents, 92% said these soft skills were more important than technical skills, and 80% said they contributed more to the success of a company or project.

As you are reading through this chapter, I encourage you to mark up this book with notes about those you consider your superpowers and where there may be gaps. I'm willing to bet that you will identify with many of these qualities and have used them in your lives.

Identifying your strengths and areas for growth is incredibly helpful in determining your leadership journey. Knowing what you're good at boosts your confidence and helps you build stronger connections with others. Leaning into your superpowers helps you decide what actions will give you the greatest impact. It's time to come out of the shadows and step into your power.

So, grab your highlighter, markers, multi-colored pens or pencils, or crayons and see how many qualities on this list make you naturally you. If you believe all the research on leadership skills, which I do because I have seen the results, I hope you'll come to the same conclusion I have: you have the potential to be an amazing change agent.

Problem Solving: Turning Challenges into Opportunities

Women are natural problem-solvers. Whether navigating the complexities of family life, managing professional responsibilities, or balancing both, women often approach challenges with creativity and resourcefulness. This stems from our ability to look at situations holistically, taking into account emotional, relational, and practical aspects of challenges. How many of you are the keepers of the calendars for your families? Sometimes it's like a puzzle—trying to fit all the pieces together.

How many of you have side gigs? Many women turn hobbies into successful businesses to solve personal financial challenges or create new opportunities outside of corporate life that provide more flexibility and autonomy. In 2022, women founded almost half of all new businesses, and more than 47% of entrepreneurs are women.

Have you ever been asked to resolve conflicts at work, with friends, or in your family? Who in your community, workplace, or children's school usually organizes events? More often than not it's women. Why? We figure things out and get things done!

As Margaret Thatcher once said, "If you want something said, ask a man; if you want something done, ask a woman." She was the first woman British prime minister and stayed in office longer than any other prime minister during the 20th century. She knew what she was talking about.

Additionally, women leaders frequently excel in collaborative problem-solving. We engage diverse perspectives to arrive at innovative solutions. I know I have probably overused the phrase "Let's see what everyone says," but I think it leads to better decisions. Our capacity to combine intuition with analytical thinking allows us to approach problems strategically while considering the human impact. This blend of logic and empathy makes problem-solving highly effective, especially in complex scenarios where decisions should consider the needs of those involved.

We often problem-solve without even realizing we are doing it. But I think all of you should be putting a check next to this quality.

Communication: Inspiring Connection

Effective communication lies at the heart of great leadership, and women often bring a unique strength to this skill. Women tend to listen actively, speak with authenticity, and adapt their communication style to suit the needs of their audience. These traits make them approachable and relatable leaders who inspire trust and engagement. Additionally, women often foster spaces of psychological safety, where individuals feel comfortable expressing their ideas, challenges, and feedback. We encourage all voices to contribute to the conversation. Have you ever noticed someone not really engaged in the conversation and asked them to share their thoughts?

When practicing active listening, we not only pay attention to the words and intonation, but we also watch the nonverbal cues, body language, and facial expressions when seeking to understand the perspectives of others. I can almost hear my mom saying, "Don't use that tone of voice with me." I know I have even mimicked this phrase with my daughter on occasion.

Listening, whether active or not, also creates space for more candid dialogue.

We know we can't talk to our partner the same way we talk to children. We also recognize how different friends need to be approached and communicated with differently. This may seem intuitive, but is really a high level communication skill.

Women also tend to be better at what experts call empathetic listening, which means considering and trying to understand other peoples' perspectives during a conversation. It's like the phrase "try to walk in their shoes." If you've ever comforted someone by using words like "I can see why you'd be upset" or "I can only imagine how hard this must be," you are using this powerful skill. You are listening beyond just words to the real emotions and meaning of what someone is saying. You are creating a space where people feel heard and validated. By truly listening to and valuing others, you demonstrate respect, care, and a commitment to better relationships.

This skill is essential to leaders because it builds trust, inspires a culture of collaboration and inclusion, and empowers people to work together towards a common goal.

Right now, I'm imagining you highlighting this skill, too, because you have probably at some time practiced active and/or empathetic listening with a parent, child, loved one, friend, co-worker, etc.

Empathy: The Heart of Leadership

Empathetic listening segues nicely into the next trait, empathy. Once considered a soft skill, in today's leadership paradigm, this is one of the most defining qualities of a strong leader, and women often lead with it naturally.

Sometimes people confuse sympathy with empathy. Sympathy is thought of as having pity on someone without necessarily understanding their circumstances. At its core, empathy is the ability to understand and share the feelings and perspectives of others, and in a leadership context, it means leading with humanity and emotional intelligence. (We will delve more deeply into that in Chapter 3.)

Showing interest in someone's dreams and hopes, and compassion for their circumstances, builds and strengthens relationships, improves communication, and inspires others to reach higher and thrive.

If you've ever comforted a friend or coworker experiencing a hardship by taking the time to listen to their frustrations, sadness, fears, etc., you are practicing empathy. If you've noticed someone standing on the sidelines and warmly invite them to join a group conversation, making them feel seen and included—that's empathy.

Empathy in women is shaped by a combination of innate tendencies, socialization, and life experiences. While many women may seem naturally empathetic, it's also a skill that can be developed and refined through intentional practice and effort. This blend of nature and nurture makes empathy a powerful trait for women in all roles, particularly in leadership.

Creative and Visionary Thinking: Seeing Beyond the Horizon

Creative thinking is often linked to problem-solving, although it is also an important element of visionary thinking. So, what is visionary thinking? It's the ability to imagine what the future could look like and find creative ways to get there. It's about seeing possibilities that others might miss and connecting today's actions to tomorrow's opportunities. Visionary thinkers don't just focus on immediate challenges, but seek new opportunities for creating a better future. Women are often great at this because they naturally think about the big picture while considering the needs and perspectives of others. We're good at balancing creativity with practicality, which helps us come up with solutions that work for everyone. We have the capacity to combine emotional intelligence, adaptability, and strategic insight. Our holistic approach enables us to consider diverse perspectives, assess challenges through multiple lenses, and create inclusive, forward-thinking solutions.

Have you ever organized a fundraiser to meet a community need? If you were raising small children and feeling isolated, did you set up a moms' group?

Your actions are the result of imagining something better—visionary thinking!

Visionary thinking requires both creativity and courage, and women often excel at blending these qualities. Sometime in your life, you have probably dreamed big and inspired others to move toward a shared goal. That makes you a visionary and amazing leader and changemaker.

Adaptability: Thriving Amid Change

Adaptability is a cornerstone of leadership in today's fast-paced world, and women often excel in this area. How many times have you pivoted in life? I was seriously contemplating going back to school to study medicine when my Brazilian husband (who was a doctor) decided we were moving to Brazil. My social conditioning urged me to say okay. His needs and the financial future of our family were often more important. Please don't judge me—the norms were different in the late 70s. And, although I never became a doctor, the move started me on my life journey of adventures and personal growth, —and I had my wonderful, amazing daughter. I actually enjoyed living in Brazil—

the people, the lifestyle, a better work/life balance, the food, and most of all, the caipirinhas (a lime concoction that I still drink).

Throughout history and even today, women are constantly redefining their roles and identities. We juggle families, parenting, care-giving, homemaking, having a social life, self-care, etc. We face the challenge of being recognized as human beings first, rather than being defined solely by our gender. These diverse challenges often require us to pivot and adjust even when our inner critic might be blasting us with the imposter syndrome messaging. It's no wonder that we learn to embrace change and innovation. We adapt and modify our plans, decisions, or approaches when we are faced with changing circumstances, new information, or perspectives. (Remember that active and empathetic listening—we hear and consider the ideas of others.)

Have you ever organized a dinner party and learned that some people who originally said they weren't available are now coming? You reset the dinner table or order more party trays to accommodate the change. That's adaptability!

Work-life balance, cross-cultural navigation, psychological flexibility and resilience are all important elements of adaptability that women tend to excel at. And adaptability is considered one of the most critical leadership skills.

Delegation: Empowering Through Trust

Delegation is not about giving up responsibility, but about empowering others to contribute their best work. Women leaders often excel at this because of their ability to build trust and nurture talent.

Now, this is a tricky one. I know that I am not always great at delegating. Sometimes I feel I have to do it all to prove my worth.

I finally changed my perspective and realized that delegating allowed others to contribute and often stretch their growth. But I also learned that delegation is not just about dividing work. It's about giving people tasks in a way that aligns with their abilities, interests, and capacity. I never asked my daughter to sharpen knives when she was 10. Nor would I ask a friend who loves creative tasks to take on the logistics of a project.

Since women tend to be emotionally attuned to others, we are able to recognize individual strengths, motivations, and preferences. This allows us to delegate tasks in a way that aligns with people's abilities and interests, ensuring they feel valued and capable.

By delegating effectively, women leaders not only maximize productivity but also create opportunities for others to grow and excel.

Conflict Resolution: Turning Differences into Strengths

Conflict is inevitable in any leadership role, but women often approach it with emotional intelligence, diplomacy, and a solutions-oriented mindset. Our active and empathetic listening skills equip us with the capacity to understand multiple perspectives, and mediate with fairness.

Whether it's social conditioning or inherent strengths, we tend to understand and address the emotional undercurrents of conflicts. This emotional intelligence enables us to connect with others, making it easier to find common ground and strive for resolutions that benefit all parties.

We are also conditioned to be peacemakers. Have you ever had to calm down family arguments—trying to find a solution that appeases everyone? Or have you had to find a solution for two children who want to play with the same toy at the same time?

Or have you stepped in to mediate a conversation between two colleagues at work who aren't talking to each other because they can't agree on the best way to approach a project?

If so, you are honing your skills in managing and resolving conflicts effectively. We tend to prioritize relationships so we often will ask those in the conflict what it is they really want, or how they would resolve an argument. Then we brainstorm to develop solutions that are mutually acceptable by encouraging each to consider the perspectives of the other.

Women tend to prioritize maintaining relationships, which drives us to resolve conflicts in a way that works for everyone involved and fosters long-term collaboration. This ability to transform conflict into collaboration strengthens team cohesion and trust.

Collaboration: The Power of Working Together

Collaboration is an essential leadership skill. Women tend to place natural emphasis on inclusion, empathy, shared decision-making, and empowerment, which makes them exceptional at fostering collaboration. We create spaces where diverse talents are harnessed, relationships are strengthened, and group achievements are celebrated.

Women are more likely to share power rather than wielding it over others. This approach creates a sense of respect, where everyone feels empowered to contribute their best. By breaking down hierarchies, women cultivate trust and a sense of belonging within their groups. This bonding is essential to motivating others toward a common goal—an important element of leadership.

I've always said that I brainstorm better in groups. Using the collective brain power of a group and giving people the opportunity to give input to decisions increases buy-in and investment in the outcomes of members of a group. I understand that diversity is an asset, and by weaving together different talents and perspectives, we can achieve goals that are more innovative and well-rounded.

I also think that women excel at balancing work with emotional well-being, whether volunteering on a project or leading a team at work. Have you ever used check-ins or provided snacks or refreshments at a meeting? If we can't have a bit of fun while working, what's the point?

Because we tend to naturally emphasize inclusion, empathy, and empowerment, we can create spaces where diverse talents are harnessed, relationships are strengthened, and collective achievements are celebrated—an approach that benefits teams, organizations, relationships, and communities.

At this point, I hope you are seeing that these traits don't usually stand alone, but are interconnected. When you reflect on those that you consider your strengths, I hope you recognize how they are linked within you.

Courage: Leading with Boldness

"Each time a woman stands up for herself, without knowing it possibly, without claiming it, she stands up for all women."
— Maya Angelou

Leadership requires courage—courage to stand up and speak out, to take risks, and be seen. Throughout history, women have been pushing their way to the forefront to challenge norms, shape societies and drive change.

The suffrage movement was led by courageous women. Ruby Bridges braved hostile crowds to be the first black student to attend an all-white Southern elementary school. Helen Keller, a blind and deaf girl who everyone thought was hopeless –went on to graduate from college and become an author, lecturer, and activist for disability rights. Dolores Huerta, daughter of a farm-worker, became a teacher and then an activist who cofounded of the National Farm Workers Association (NFWA). Malala Yousafzai is a Pakistani female education activist, film and television producer, and the 2014 Nobel Peace Prize laureate at the age of 17. At 15, she was shot in the head three times for advocating for education for girls in Pakistan.

These women had the courage to challenge systemic barriers in order to live with integrity—aligning their personal values with their behavior. Systemic barriers or inequities are obstacles embedded within policies, practices, cultures, or institutions that disproportionately disadvantage certain groups of people. These barriers arise from the way systems are designed and operate, often reflecting historical inequities and societal biases. They are not isolated incidents but are ingrained in the frameworks of organizations and societies.

They challenged outdated practices, were willing to be innovative, and took risks. As Helen Keller is famous for saying, "Life is either a daring adventure or nothing at all."

Women lead courageously in countless ways, often without fanfare or recognition. Their acts of bravery and leadership transform lives and communities, showing that courage isn't always loud—it's found in the quiet, determined actions that make a difference.

Have you ever volunteered at a food bank or other community nonprofit, organized community or school events, or mentored young people? Your willingness to serve embodies everyday courage. You lead with compassion and a vision for a better, more connected community.

I went back to school to get a Master's degree when I was 59. Was I nervous, scared, and asking myself if I was being ridiculous (that saboteur in my brain)? Absolutely, but I aspired to work with women globally and needed that credential to accomplish my dream.

Change takes a lot of courage. It means facing your fears, navigating challenges, and staying open to growing in ways you might not have expected. Change is often met with resistance. You know that old saying "better the devil you know than the devil you don't know." Many people don't like uncertainty... not knowing the ripple effects of change. Or they're afraid the power dynamic might shift—that power is a zero-sum game, a pie and if I share my power with you, I have less.

On the other hand, leaders embrace change. I'm known for using the phrase, "you either embrace change and evolve or become a dinosaur—and they're extinct." And women, with their penchant for adaptability, creative problem-solving, and visionary thinking, have the courage to change.

Courage inspires others, creating ripple effects of bold, principled leadership. You're stronger than you realize, and every step you take toward transformation is a powerful act of bravery.

Resilience: Rising Strong

Resilience is all about finding the strength to recover from life's challenges, and women leaders show this every day through their persistence and determination. The ups and downs— whether in work or personal life—help build that inner strength, which makes their leadership even more impactful.

Women are inherently resilient. We adapt, endure, and thrive in the face of challenges. This resilience is shaped by a combination of experiences, social dynamics, and personal strengths. We often juggle multiple roles—leaders, caregivers, professionals, and community members—requiring us to constantly adapt and reprioritize. This ability to balance diverse demands strengthens our capacity to handle change and challenges.

Our relationship bonds with family, friends, and colleagues give us emotional strength and encouragement during difficult times.

Our emotional intelligence allows us to process challenges, manage stress, and adapt. Self-awareness and empathy are such powerful tools—they give us the strength to handle tough emotions and navigate even the most complicated situations.

When overcoming hardships, women often find healthy ways to move forward by reframing challenges as opportunities for growth, drawing strength from their experiences, and leaning on supportive networks. Rather than dwelling on these hardships and allowing them to be boulders weighing them down, women tend to view them as stepping stones for growth.

Women are more likely to show their vulnerability as a way to find connection and healing. When we share our stories—whether with close friends, family, or a larger community—it helps us grow and make sense of our experiences, giving us strength and resilience.

Whether you advance in a career in a male-dominated industry, enduring bias and skepticism, or leave the corporate world to build your own business, pursuing new passions and finding success in a different field, conquer a devastating illness or seek counseling for your mental wellness—you are showing resilience.

The act of moving through difficulties, discovering meaningful ways to integrate them into your life journey, and growing from them is resilience.

My mom used to say that no one gets out of life unscathed. I know you have had your share of hard knocks. You are reading this book because you survived and thrived—you are resilient.

Trust Building: The Foundation of Leadership

Trust is the foundation of any relationship, personal or professional. We know when we feel it, and the pain and disappointment of losing it.

As Lady Gaga said in her Harvard Commencement speech, "Trust is like a mirror, you can fix it if it's broken, but you can still see the cracks." So, building and maintaining trust is essential to being in relationships and working with others.

Women have a natural talent for building trust because they are genuine, care deeply about others, and consistently follow through on what they say.

I'm not sure if it was my father or Dr. Seuss who said this first, but in part, consistency is "I meant what I said, and I said what I meant." Knowing that someone lives by their word nurtures trust. Living by your word establishes trust because it demonstrates integrity, proving that you respect others enough to honor your commitments. Over time, people know they can trust not just your words but your intentions and actions.

We tend to use our listening skills to understand different perspectives, which helps people feel heard, valued, and safe to share opinions. This combination of emotional intelligence, genuine care for others, inclusion, and fairness makes us exceptional at earning and maintaining trust in both personal and professional relationships.

For women, trust and vulnerability are deeply connected, forming the foundation of supportive relationships. When we share our stories, open up about challenges, or lean on others during tough times, we are creating trust. Vulnerability isn't a weakness—it's an act of courage and strength that builds deeper bonds and encourages others to be just as open. Through this balance of giving and receiving, we foster relationships and even communities of connection, empathy, and mutual support through trust.

Trust is essential to leadership. I imagine you have had an experience where you joined someone on a project because you "believed in them." I also imagine that you have distanced yourself from someone you don't trust.

You might be seeing a pattern here—these traits are intertwined. Having empathy, communications that open spaces and value others, and showing vulnerability all contribute to building trust. And women tend to apply many of these qualities as leaders and inspire connection, confidence, and a willingness for others to join in on their journey for change.

Personal Growth: Committing to Lifelong Learning

Great leaders are lifelong learners, and women often embody this mindset by continually seeking opportunities to grow both personally and professionally. We understand that leadership isn't about having all the answers but about being open to new ideas, perspectives, and ways of thinking. We approach learning with curiosity and see feedback not as criticism, but as an opportunity to become better—for ourselves and others in our lives.

This openness to evolving and adapting allows women to navigate challenges with creativity and determination, while striving to enhance our impact and lift up those around us. Whether it's through deep reflection, seeking new knowledge, or learning from the experiences of others, we embrace growth as a way to lead with greater purpose and care. By showing that leadership is a journey of learning, we inspire others to believe in their own ability to grow and thrive.

I listed personal growth last because it depends on all the other qualities in this chapter—our self-reflection to identify our values and who we are; our active and empathetic listening to learn from others; our adaptability; having the courage to quiet that voice of the imposter syndrome to trust in our capabilities to venture on our journey of change; communication that inspires others to join our pursuits... These all require personal growth.

This commitment to growth makes women highly adaptable, able to navigate change and challenges with flexibility and creativity. Have you ever attended a leadership workshop; used a setback like losing your job to reinvent yourself; joined a book club or other social activities for connection; gone back to school or pursued other opportunities to gain knowledge and learn new skills; committed to counseling, journaling, or meditation for your mental well-being? The list of pursuing personal growth goes on and on. And, if you've done any of these things, you have engaged in personal growth. All these pursuits unlock your potential for leadership. Remember, potential is just unharnessed power—those superpowers you are discovering and awakening.

As you grow, you will lead.

Conclusion: The Future is Bright

All these leadership qualities are beautifully intertwined, each one weaving into the other like threads in a tapestry—empathy that deepens connection, communication that builds trust, collaboration that ignites possibility, and visioning that inspires hope.

The traits that make women exceptional leaders—problem solving, visionary thinking, adaptability, delegation, conflict resolution, collaboration, courage, resilience, trust building, and personal growth— together form a powerful foundation for leadership that is inclusive, impactful, and transformative.

As more women step into leadership roles, they bring with them a unique blend of skills that inspire teams, drive innovation, and create lasting change. By embracing and celebrating these qualities, women not only excel as leaders but also redefine what it means to lead in today's world.

If you haven't yet, get your free downloadable companion Workbook at cathyholt.com/unstoppableworkbook to go deeper on the chapter, write down your thoughts, and consider these takeaways and action steps.

Key Takeaways

1. Leadership is Evolving: Traditional leadership focused on control and results. Modern leadership values empathy, adaptability, and inclusivity—qualities women naturally excel in.

2. The Power of Soft Skills: Traits once dismissed as "soft skills" (e.g., communication, empathy, adaptability) are now recognized as essential for effective leadership.

3. Women Are Exceptional Problem-Solvers: Women approach challenges holistically, using creativity, collaboration, and resourcefulness to find solutions.

4. Communication is Foundational: Active and empathetic listening, combined with authentic expression, fosters trust, collaboration, and connection.

5. Empathy is Central: Women lead with humanity, understanding others' perspectives to build stronger relationships and inspire change.

6. Visionary Thinking: Women balance creativity and practicality to imagine and achieve a better future.

7. Adaptability Builds Resilience: Women's ability to pivot and navigate change strengthens their leadership effectiveness.

8. Collaboration Over Hierarchy: Women emphasize inclusion and shared power, creating environments where everyone thrives.

9. Courage, Trust, and Resilience: Women lead boldly, build trust through integrity, and rise strong in the face of challenges.

10. Leadership is a Journey of Growth: Women's commitment to lifelong learning enhances their ability to lead with purpose and adaptability.

Action Steps to Apply the Chapter's Insights

1. Identify Your Strengths and Gaps:

    a. Reflect on the traits discussed and note your leadership superpowers. Use a journal or highlight them in the text.

    b. Identify areas where you want to grow and create a plan to strengthen those traits.

2. Practice Empathy and Communication:

    a. Engage in active and empathetic listening during conversations.

b. Adapt your communication style based on the needs of your audience to build stronger connections.

3. Embrace Change and Innovate:

a. Seek opportunities to adapt and innovate in your personal and professional life.

b. Approach challenges with curiosity and creativity, envisioning the possibilities beyond obstacles.

4. Foster Collaboration and Trust:

a. Build inclusive spaces where diverse perspectives are valued and leveraged for collective success.

b. Be consistent in your actions and words to nurture trust with those you lead.

5. Develop Your Leadership Mindset:

a. Pursue personal growth through workshops, mentorship, or self-reflection.

b. Quiet the voice of self-doubt by recognizing your accomplishments and the impact of your leadership.

Call to Action: Step Into Your Power

The time is now to awaken your leadership potential and embrace your unique strengths. You already possess the qualities needed to inspire, guide, and create lasting change. Reflect on the traits outlined in this chapter, celebrate your superpowers, and take actionable steps to grow as a leader.

The future depends on leaders who value connection, inclusivity, and resilience—leaders like you. Begin today by leaning into your strengths, nurturing your growth, and stepping boldly into your role as a changemaker. You have the power to transform lives and build a brighter, more equitable world.

Chapter 2

Self-Reflection

Perception—We may think it's our reality, but is it?

We are bombarded by thousands of messages each day. Our subconscious soaks up these messages, only transferring a limited number to our consciousness. But all these messages are creating our perceptions, our beliefs, biases, judgements—about others and ourselves.

I remember one day, my daughter came home from junior high school and announced that she was giving up on math. She wasn't good at it and just didn't "have it in her DNA." Now, her dad is a surgeon, and I was a nerd who loved math—so even if math was determined by DNA, she should have been good at it. I asked her where she got this idea from, and she proudly announced that "everyone knows girls aren't built for math." How did she come up with this limiting belief?

Coming of age in the 70s, I heard many limiting beliefs about women and girls. I even bought into some of them, like women were supposed to be trim and fit and blonds had more fun. Heck, I even let my high school boyfriend beat me at tennis because his feelings were more important than mine.

Where did I get these ideas from? Definitely not at home. My mom and dad were raising their 3 daughters to be independent individuals first and foremost.

According to studies, our brains process about 70,000 thoughts per day. Yet only about 5% of those make it to our conscious mind. The rest are swirling around in there impacting the ideas and conclusions we come up with. To top it off, our brains are wired with what neuroscientific researchers call negativity bias. We tend to remember negative experiences and thoughts more than positive ones. They posit that this bias is based on evolution and survival like remembering that touching fire hurts us, while touching cool water doesn't.

Regardless of why negativity bias occurs, it means that we are all more apt to dwell on shortcomings instead of successes. We will focus on our faults rather than our strengths. A friend of mine who is a body positivity coach challenges every woman she works with to look in the mirror after a bath or shower, and find something about their body that they like. How hard is that—it was for me.

Her process started with self-reflection. She was asking us to ignore all those messages about a socially conceived perfect body and think positively about what nature gave us. Despite all my sags, bags, and wrinkles, I recognized that I was relatively physically fit and able. Can I run a 10k like I used to? Absolutely not! But I can walk for hours sightseeing and window shopping in New York City. And I was thankful for that. Rather than focusing on my negatives, I was focusing on my positive attributes.

The Importance of Self-Reflection for Women

Self-reflection is of utmost importance to our well-being and personal growth. But so often, women are juggling so many roles and responsibilities that we put ourselves at the bottom of our priority lists.

Honestly, the only way to truly get to know yourself is to spend some quality time together—after all, you're stuck with you 24/7, so you might as well make it a good relationship! Self-reflection is the art of turning your focus inward, exploring your thoughts, emotions, behaviors, and motivations with curiosity. It's about stepping outside the noise of daily life, suspending judgment, and uncovering new insights about who you are and what drives you.

Taking time to reflect on your life is like giving yourself a moment to breathe, refocus, and realign with what truly matters to you. You are able to reconnect with your core values and uncover your unique strengths. You gain a deeper understanding of your dreams, thoughts, and aspirations. With this self-knowledge, you can assess what truly matters to you and align your action with what matters. In the midst of juggling responsibilities and meeting expectations, it's easy to lose sight of ourselves. Taking time to reflect allows us to pause, listen to our inner voice, and ask: Am I living authentically? Am I showing up in the way I want for myself and others?

By understanding what drives us, we can set healthy boundaries and step into leadership roles in our own lives. You will start to prioritize what's important to you and make intentional choices aligned with your values and that "feel right."

With this self-awareness you can show up honestly and genuinely, staying true to your values, beliefs, and personality without putting on a facade to fit others' expectations. It involves being transparent about who you are, showing vulnerability by owning both your strengths and imperfections, and engaging with others in a way that reflects your true self. Showing up authentically fosters trust and connection, as it allows people to interact with the real you rather than a carefully curated version of yourself.

Science now tells us that there is a connection between our brain and our gut called the gut-brain axis. Both are nervous systems communicating with each other. Often, when a decision aligns with your values and goals, you might feel a calming or affirming sensation in your gut, while a decision that goes against them might trigger discomfort or unease. All this means that your gut feelings can provide great insights. And balancing those feelings with a strong foundation of values and aspirations should result in well-rounded decision-making.

For women, self-reflection is about more than just personal growth—it's about empowerment. It's a practice that helps us embrace our worth and deepen our confidence. And, in a world that often demands we put others first, self-reflection is a radical act of self-care. It's how we refill our emotional well and ensure we have the energy, clarity, and strength to show up fully and create a life that aligns with those things we value— for ourselves, in our relationships, and our communities.

Women often encounter unique barriers to self-reflection, rooted in the demands and expectations placed on them by society, work, and family. The constant pull of responsibilities can leave little room for moments of stillness, making it challenging to prioritize introspection.

Challenges to self-reflection:

Societal norms

Many women navigate societal norms that encourage them to focus on others' needs before their own, leading to feelings of guilt or selfishness when setting aside time for themselves. Balancing roles as caregivers, professionals, and community members leaves little time for personal reflection. The superwoman myth is just that—a myth. The idea was popularized by Helen Gurley Brown, editor of Cosmopolitan, in her 1982 book Having It All. Maybe she could have it all because she had a huge team to get everything done.

My team is often me, myself, and I, and we need to recruit more team members. I will admit, I fell into the superwoman trap. I worked, wanted to be the perfect party hostess wife, was a community volunteer, and an attentive mother and daughter. I was in charge of the active family social and travel calendar. Our schedule was always full. One summer I drove a three-horse trailer 11,000 miles to get my daughter and her mounts to horse shows as she pursued an Olympic dream. I lived near enough to my parents to help behind the scenes of their social activities and family gatherings. I joined the sandwich generation as I was the primary care support for both my daughter and my parents. And I also found time to exercise and "feel the burn" to meet societies standards of a Texas doctor's wife. I was so busy running a never-ending marathon with no finish line in sight, I didn't even realize introspection was a thing. Fortunately, life experiences taught me that being a superwoman was another way for society to get more out of women and leave less for themselves. And I started exploring who I was and really wanted to be.

Some things haven't changed that much. In this fast-paced modern life, self-reflection might feel like a luxury rather than a necessity. Our culture of constant productivity discourages pausing for introspection. In our hustle-bustle world, having a packed schedule is glorified, while slowing down is seen as laziness or inefficiency. Balancing professional responsibilities, caregiving, and household duties leaves little personal time. We measure worth by achievements like promotions, income, or milestones rather than internal satisfaction. Because communications are instantaneous, we are pressured to respond to emails, messages, or work tasks immediately, even during our personal or family time. Women taking time for themselves often hear the message that they are being selfish.

Times of Adversity

For women whose lives are filled with responsibilities, struggles, or uncertainty, the idea of pausing to think about values, strengths, or aspirations seems impractical. But in reality, it can be a lifeline—a small, quiet way to reclaim a sense of self amid adversity.

Reflection doesn't have to be a long elaborate process. Ask yourself, "What do I need right now to feel more grounded?" or "What's one small thing I'm proud of today?" These moments of introspection help reconnect us with our inner strength and remind us that we are more than our current circumstances.

In a 2-year period of my adult life, I was faced with more challenges than I ever imagined.

During my 47th trip around the sun, my mom's battle with COPD came to an end one difficult night in the hospital, where I had to remind my grieving father of her wish for no heroic measures— a heartbreaking moment that left a deep mark on my soul. Her passing was followed by the devastation of my 18-year-old daughter's stroke, which left her paralyzed on one side and facing major heart surgery while fighting for her life. During her recovery, we were blindsided again when her father decided to leave, prioritizing himself over his family. His exit and absence during our most vulnerable time compounded the chaos, as I navigated grief and accompanied my daughter on her recovery journey.

I was incredibly fortunate to have friends who stepped in to help care for my daughter and give me much-needed moments of quiet. During that time, I was able to step out of my head and into my heart, allowing me to reflect deeply on my life, my choices, and what truly mattered to me. I blocked out the noise of expectations and focused on what I valued and how I wanted to live. These moments of self-reflection allowed me to be present and show up authentically in my daughter's recovery and make life-altering decisions based on my values and aspirations about my future. I went back to school for a Master's degree and started working with grassroots and community based women around the world.

During difficult times, self-reflection can be an act of resilience— a way to honor who you are and what you've endured. It's not about fixing everything at once but about finding those sparks of clarity and self-worth that keep you moving forward, one step at a time.

A young woman, Andrea, who has experienced much adversity in her life, shared with me her reflection on being the leader of her own life. Through her journey of self-reflection, she realized that "How my life is going to end up is my responsibility solely. It's all about the choices I make. With the consistency of choosing what aligns with you, in time, you will see that you are leading and impacting your own and so many other lives. It's beautiful, and I am very grateful for this journey."

It's scary

Reflecting on your life can be unnerving. It might surface uncomfortable memories, which can be daunting to confront. For some, the fear of acknowledging their flaws, weaknesses, or past choices may discourage deeper introspection. Sometimes, we avoid reflecting because it might bring up questions or feelings we're not ready to face.

All of these are possibilities. And it takes courage to visit and sit with discomfort. The purpose of self-reflection is not to dwell on past mistakes or criticize ourselves, but to create space for learning and growth. When approached through a compassionate lens with kindness and curiosity, self-reflection becomes an empowering process that turns missteps into stepping stones in the journey of self-discovery and achievement. It's not about the would've, should've, could've conversation with ourselves that often replays like a continuous reel in our heads. It's about asking yourself, "What went wrong, what could I have done differently, and what valuable lessons can I learn from these lived experiences?" This growth mindset will help identify opportunities for improvement and build resilience.

Remember that concept of negativity bias—how our brain tends to focus on negative aspects of an experience instead of the positive? When learning from your past, it's important to also ask, "Was it really as bad as I thought it was, or did something good actually come out of the experience? Did it change me for the better?" These often sound like clichés, but looking at setbacks as opportunities to learn rather than failures help us travel our pathway to being our best selves.

I feel the need to digress a moment here. We all get caught up on words like success and failure. They are often presented as opposites when they really are not. They are deeply interconnected and are part of the same journey. We assign failure when we don't reach a goal or the result of our actions doesn't give us an expected outcome. In reality, we should be look at the result as a lesson in how not to do something and create a new pathway to attaining our goals. Rather than labeling our efforts as successes or failures, we need to look at the discoveries made and the problem-solving skills learned.

As Thomas Edison famously said, "'I have not failed 1,000 times. I have successfully discovered 1,000 ways to not make a light bulb."

Additionally, growth requires that you set goals outside your comfort zone—those stretch goals that you can't do yet. That should come with the understanding that you might not reach that goal on the first or even second try and that there will likely be road bumps on the journey. (We'll delve more into that in Chapter 10.)

For now, I want you to give yourself grace during your self-reflection for those unpleasant memories or perceived "failures." Because, in reality, everything you learned through those missteps helped shape the person you have become. Understanding those mistakes improved your decision-making and ability to conquer adversity. They helped you learn about your strengths and areas for growth while eventually boosting your belief in your abilities to move forward in life. Rather than being stuck in the pain of setbacks, self-reflection empowers us to use those experiences as a foundation for future successes, fostering self-awareness and confidence in our ability to navigate this rollercoaster called life.

So, remember:

- Nobody gets it right all the time.
- Mistakes and setbacks are part of being human and part of the journey to growth.
- Perfection isn't the goal, progress is.
- Focus on what you can learn, rather than judging yourself for how it turned out.
- You're not defined by one moment or outcome; you're defined by how you grow and move forward.
- Acknowledge the courage it took to try, even if things didn't go as planned. That effort alone is something to be proud of.

As Confucius is credited with saying, "Our greatest glory is not in never falling, but in getting up every time we do."

It's amazing how we can be so much more forgiving of others than we can of ourselves. I know I have to constantly remind myself to not be my biggest critic and now try to replace that criticism with self-care because compassion towards yourself builds the emotional foundation to keep trying and learning. Self-reflection in the face of trauma

I will not pretend to know all the challenges of self-reflection after significant trauma. Self-reflection after trauma is a courageous act. It can be a delicate process that requires patience, intentionality, and a focus on healing. Approach it with gentleness and self-understanding, remembering that it's okay to seek help and take your time. Healing is a journey, and your willingness to reflect is already a step toward reclaiming your sense of self and peace.

Uncertainty

Another barrier to self-reflection might be the uncertainty about how to begin or where to start. The concept may feel vague or overwhelming, especially if you have never been encouraged to explore your inner world. You may question its value or worry that focusing on yourself will uncover uncomfortable truths or amplify self-doubt. This perception fosters doubt that self-reflection is necessary and can give rise to a feeling that it is too daunting to undertake. These beliefs distance you from the benefits of clarity and personal growth that introspection offers. Even small glimpses of self-awareness can guide better decisions and stronger relationships.

Overcoming these barriers often requires reframing self-reflection as an act of self-care and empowerment rather than a task or luxury. Without understanding the transformative power of self-reflection, it can seem like an unnecessary indulgence.

But knowing yourself is an essential foundation for growth and meaningful change, empowering you to navigate life with greater confidence and purpose. By embracing the process, you discover that self-reflection is not about dwelling on the past but about learning, growing, and creating a path toward your best self.

Encouraging Self-Reflection for Women

Creating opportunities and normalizing self-reflection as a vital part of personal and professional growth can help women embrace this practice. Small steps, such as journaling, meditating, or setting aside quiet moments, can lead to significant transformations, empowering women to lead more authentic and fulfilled lives.

Why self-reflection matters for women:

1. **Get Clear on What You Want** – Understand what's most important and make decisions that feel right.
2. **Build Confidence** – Appreciate your achievements and see how far you've come.
3. **Recharge Emotionally** – Process emotions, let go of stress, and build inner strength.
4. **Create Healthy Boundaries** – Know your limits and find ways to honor them.
5. **Find Purpose** – Discover what excites you and fuels your passion.

Making Self-Reflection a Habit

It's easy to underestimate how much a little quiet time for yourself can make a big difference in how you show up in your life.

Taking even a few minutes a day to reflect can do wonders. Whether it's journaling, going for a walk, or simply sitting quietly with your thoughts, self-reflection is a gift you give to yourself. It helps you feel more grounded, connected, and ready to take on whatever comes next. When you take time to tune into your own needs and dreams, you're not only helping yourself—you're setting the stage to show up more fully for the people and things you care about.

Self-reflection is essential to the leadership journey.

Leadership begins with understanding yourself—your values, skills, and strengths. You will see that you have what it takes to lead. This process gives you the opportunity to identify your leadership superpowers and skills that are now considered valuable to take charge and be a change agent. Using this self-awareness of your experiences, accomplishments, and missteps, you can also determine where to focus on areas of personal growth and improvement.

Self-reflection is a transformative tool that strengthens emotional intelligence by encouraging you to process your feelings and understand how these emotions influence your relationships and interactions with others. It also sharpens self-awareness and enhances your ability to recognize the impact of your decisions, motivations, and actions. By consciously examining your values, strengths, and areas for growth, you cultivate more intentional and effective leadership.

This deeper awareness improves empathy, communication, and connection with others, allowing you to share your vision or goals. When you understand yourself, you're better equipped to show up authentically, build trust, and create a culture of collaboration.

Aligning your purpose—the "why" behind your decision to step up and speak out—enables you to make value-driven decisions informed by experience and continuous learning.

Reflecting on setbacks and challenges helps you, as a leader, find lessons in adversity, strengthening your ability to bounce back stronger and be better prepared for the future. It fosters a mindset that views mistakes as learning opportunities rather than failures.

Regularly checking in with yourself, your thoughts, and your actions ensures you stay true to your course and your core values. Knowing yourself helps you stay humble and heart-centered by encouraging you to acknowledge your imperfections, learn from your experiences, and remain grounded in empathy and authenticity as a person and a leader.

In short, self-reflection is not a one-time activity but an ongoing practice that enables leaders to grow, adapt, and lead effectively. It transforms leadership from mere management into a journey of purpose-driven influence and impact.

Let self-reflection become one of your superpowers. Don't put it off for "later." If you do, you'll miss the profound opportunities it offers to refine your leadership and cultivate a life of intention and impact. Make it a cornerstone of your journey, and you'll continually uncover new depths of growth and possibility.

> *"You may encounter many defeats, but you must not be defeated. In fact, it may be necessary to encounter the defeats, so you can know who you are, what you can rise from, how you can still come out of it."*
> - Maya Angelou

Exercise: Engaging in regular self-reflection is a powerful practice for women seeking personal growth and fulfillment. By setting aside time to thoughtfully consider your experiences, emotions, and choices, you can gain deeper insights into your values, strengths, and areas for improvement. This process not only enhances self-awareness but also empowers you to make intentional decisions that align with your authentic self.

According to the International Institute for Management Development in Lausanne, Switzerland, the five clear steps that you can follow to evolve your process of self-reflection and grow as a leader are:

1. Notice what you notice.
2. Feel the emotions before you start thinking about it.
3. Question your own explanations for your feelings.
4. Identify your own predictable patterns.
5. Make intentional choices to accept or change.

Self-reflection means slowing down and paying attention to your thoughts, feelings, and experiences with curiosity and without judgement.

To begin your self-reflection journey, consider asking yourself:

1. What are the moments in my life that have brought me the most joy, and what do they reveal about my passions?

2. In which situations have I felt most confident, and how can I cultivate more of these experiences?

3. What challenges have I faced, and what have they taught me about my resilience and adaptability?

4. How do I respond to stress, and what strategies can I implement to manage it more effectively?

5. What are the relationships in my life that nourish me, and how can I nurture them further?

6. What unique strengths, values, and perspectives do I bring to leadership, and how can I use them to inspire and empower others?

Reflecting on these questions can provide valuable insights into your personal journey and guide you toward a more intentional and fulfilling life. Remember, self-reflection is a continuous process that evolves with you, offering opportunities for growth and deeper understanding.

If you haven't yet, get your free downloadable companion Workbook at cathyholt.com/unstoppableworkbook to go deeper on the chapter, write down your thoughts, and consider these takeaways and action steps.

Chapter 3

Empathy and Emotional Intelligence: How Women Harness EQ to Lead with Impact

The Power of Empathy and EQ in Leadership

Women often navigate a world where emotional intelligence (also known as emotional quotient or EQ) and empathy are essential yet undervalued. In leadership, these interpersonal traits become powerful tools for building trust, fostering collaboration, and creating inclusive spaces. While traditionally dismissed as "soft skills," empathy and EQ are now recognized as critical for modern leadership, transforming how leaders inspire and connect.

Empathy: A Cornerstone of Emotional Intelligence

Empathy is the ability to step into someone else's world, imagining their feelings and experiences. It's about listening without judgment or expectations, meeting people where they are, and respecting their lived experiences. True empathy means recognizing all aspects of identity—such as gender, race, sexual identity, ability, and origin stories. You acknowledge that these have shaped their lives and that they are the experts of their lived experiences. You believe them when they share their stories.

Empathy is an essential leadership trait because it fosters trust, understanding, and meaningful connections. Leaders who demonstrate empathy can better anticipate the needs of their teams, address challenges collaboratively, and create inclusive environments where everyone feels valued. Whether empathy is due to lived experiences or social conditioning, women are uniquely prepared to excel at empathy that encourages them to listen, nurture, and prioritize relationships. These experiences equip women with the skills to understand and respond to others' emotions effectively, making them highly effective at leading with compassion and insight.

Why Women Tend to Be Empathetic:

Socialization plays a significant role. Researcher, author, and educator Jean Kilbourne has studied the impact of media and advertising for decades. In 2015, she noted that we were exposed to over 3,000 advertisements daily—and this was before social media became a dominant force. Many of these messages perpetuate stereotypes of women as caregivers, sexy objects of desire, or people who must become attractive to gain approval.

Societal narratives often encourage women to nurture, sacrifice, and prioritize others. Stories like *Beauty and the Beast* or *Casablanca* (in which Ingrid Bergman abandons Humphrey Bogart, her true love, to leave Casablanca and support her husband, a key resistance fighter against the Nazis) reinforce the trope of self-sacrifice and giving up your own aspirations as love.

Even from a young age, girls are immersed in narratives that emphasize nurturing and building relationships. While activities like playing with dolls encourage caregiving, it's equally important to expose girls to opportunities that develop skills like critical thinking, speaking up, and goal-setting to balance these influences.

While these influences can foster empathy, they also risk creating an "empathy overload." Being excessively attuned to others' emotions can have negative consequences. When we prioritize others' needs over our own, we can erode our ability to establish healthy boundaries. When we become too emotionally involved with someone who is struggling, we risk absorbing their pain and negative energy, which can ultimately harm our own well-being. This may manifest as anxiety, depression, or even physical symptoms. Personally, I often have to resist the urge to step in and fix everything—to try to take away someone's pain—because doing so can sometimes do more harm than good to both of us.

My friend, I'll call her Joan, a deeply caring and accomplished individual, stepped in to support me during the difficult period of my divorce. Her advice and guidance were invaluable, especially in the early stages when I needed help navigating legal and financial complexities. However, her ongoing desire to manage every aspect of my situation, even as I regained my footing, began to undermine my confidence and sense of independence. While her intentions came from a place of love and concern, her approach placed additional pressure on me at a time when I was already juggling the challenges of parenting a daughter with disabilities and redefining my life after the end of a partnership. Ultimately, we found a balance where her support was helpful without overshadowing my ability to make my own decisions, allowing me to reclaim my strength and autonomy.

Embracing empathy is important, especially for leaders, but there's a balance—it's okay to care deeply without carrying the weight of the world or absorbing others' emotions as your own.

Emotional Intelligence: A Framework for Leadership

Emotional intelligence is a term that is tossed around quite a bit in personal growth and leadership circles. According to the American Psychological Association, emotional intelligence is "a type of intelligence that involves the ability to process emotional information and use it in reasoning and other cognitive activities." In other words, it means that you can recognize your emotions, understand and manage them, and help others manage theirs in a supportive way. It's also knowing how to use emotions to motivate yourself and others. It enables leaders to inspire, resolve conflicts, and build strong relationships

Have you ever used your excitement and energy to rev up a group, or used empathy to help resolve a conflict? If so, you were channeling your EQ abilities. Sometimes, when my daughter was younger and I was frustrated or angry with her, I would tell her that "Mommy needs time out." I understood that I needed to separate myself from the situation to understand and manage my emotions. I didn't know it at the time, but I was using EQ.

The five key elements often identified as comprising EQ align with qualities women excel in, not because they are innate but because they are cultivated through experience and reflection.

Self-Awareness

Women leaders often reflect on their strengths, challenges, and biases, allowing them to lead authentically. They frequently demonstrate an acute understanding of how their emotions and behaviors impact others, enabling them to adjust and improve. Self-awareness is knowing yourself as a result of your self-reflection. It's usually defined as the ability to focus on yourself and how your actions, thoughts, or emotions do or don't align with your internal standards. It's not something we usually dwell on, but it's deeply ingrained in differentiating who you are.

Experts generally recognize two types of self-awareness, public and private. Public self-awareness is the ability to understand how others perceive you in social or professional settings. It involves recognizing the image you project to the world and how it aligns with societal expectations or labels, such as being seen as a professional, parent, or leader. This awareness often shapes how we adapt our behavior to fit social norms or gain acceptance in various contexts.

Have you ever asked a friend if your outfit looks professional enough right before a presentation to work colleagues? That is public self-awareness—knowing that looking the part can affect the acceptance of your message.

When I worked in politics, I initially felt intimidated by high-profile figures, but advice from seasoned women, like Ann Richards (as Texas State Treasurer before she became Governor) reminding us that "men put their pants on one leg at a time like the rest of us," helped ease my anxiety.

Private self-awareness involves introspection—looking inward to understand your thoughts, feelings, beliefs, values, abilities, and tendencies. It helps you recognize what drives your actions and emotions, enabling you to regulate your behavior and adapt to different situations. This deeper self-awareness is also where you confront and quiet the inner critic or doubts that may undermine your confidence, fostering personal growth and resilience.

My friend Pat has actually given a name to her little dealer of doubt on her shoulder and will audibly tell Charlie to "shut up and go away." To this day she won't tell us why the name Charlie, or who Charlie really was in her life.

Self-reflection and mindfulness are like two sides of the same coin. Both involve slowing down and paying attention to your thoughts, feelings, and experiences with curiosity and without judgment, but they do it in slightly different ways.

Mindfulness focuses specifically on being present in the moment, noticing thoughts, emotions, and sensations without distraction or criticism. By anchoring attention to the here and now, mindfulness helps reduce stress, quiet mental chatter, and foster inner peace.

Practices like meditation and deep breathing support mindfulness by calming the mind and training focus. In a fast-paced world where women often feel pressure to prove their worth, mindfulness offers a way to shift from constant productivity to intentional presence. This practice enhances self-awareness, emotional regulation, and clarity, empowering women leaders to navigate challenges with composure and make confident decisions.

Mindfulness also strengthens empathy (it's back) and compassion, key traits for inspiring and connecting with others, while supporting personal well-being in demanding roles. Combined with gratitude, which emphasizes appreciating life's blessings, mindfulness cultivates a positive mindset and emotional balance, enriching both leadership and personal life.
When a friend of mine was diagnosed with breast cancer, to combat the despair, fear, and 'why me' frustrations, she was grateful for her access to great doctors and medical care, her family and friends who would go with her to appointments or hold her hand or comfort her when she needed a boost, and how the diagnosis helped change her mindset, by living in the moment. Adding a daily affirmation of gratitude to your journal and contemplations shifts your mindset.

Self-Management

Self-management or regulation refers to the ability to separate emotions from your actions. More technically, it is the ability to manage your emotions, impulses, and behaviors in a thoughtful and constructive manner. It enables you to respond to situations calmly and effectively rather than reacting impulsively or emotionally. Managing emotions, especially under pressure, is a hallmark of EQ. Women's ability to self-regulate enables them to stay composed, make thoughtful decisions, and maintain focus in challenging circumstances. This skill is particularly valuable in high-stress leadership roles where measured responses are critical.

In Texas, I learned to say (with a Texas twang of course) "how nice" when I really wanted to blurt out "I really don't care." I hope I was practicing self-regulation.

It's important because it prevents you from acting based on emotions. You know those harsh words we can blurt out when we're angry or upset. My mom used to say that, "words once spoken can never be taken back and sting forever." In her generation, EQ was not even a thing, but she understood the importance of not letting emotions "get the best of you" and the power of self-regulation in maintaining trust and relationships.

Self-regulation also helps us practice adaptability (remember Chapter 1) facing change, challenges, or uncertainty with an open mind rather than reacting from emotions. It gives us the capacity to process feelings like anxiety, fear and frustration that can overwhelm us in the change process. By maintaining our calm and balance, we are likely to make better decisions and trust in our ability to bounce back from potential setbacks. Instead of panicking, we can view challenges as opportunities for learning and growth.

Let's admit it, managing our emotions is not always easy. And, that negativity bias I introduced in Chapter 1 often veers our thoughts to the dark side. For example, allowing the feelings of anger to take control of our actions sometimes happens. I once witnessed a male legislator throw a hissy fit because another legislator wouldn't support a bill he was introducing. He ranted and raved, paced, and insulted his colleague until he ran out of steam—leaving the room and slamming the door behind him. He definitely wasn't "thinking straight," building a relationship with his colleague, or making good decisions. He probably could have used a few lessons on impulse control, too.

Self-regulation also contributes to our taking responsibility for our actions—like saying sorry when we unintentional hurt someone—and keeps us on track with our goals and values when tempted to "go off the rails." Do you have a fun-loving friend that calls at the last minute to go on an afternoon adventure? Sometimes you can drop what you're doing and go, but sometimes you know you have other obligations to attend to. EQ is saying "thank you, but I can't" and getting what you need to accomplish done.

Self-regulation is a cornerstone of emotional intelligence, helping us navigate social interactions, maintain healthy relationships, and achieve personal and professional goals.

Motivation

People with emotional intelligence are often motivated by a deep passion and a drive to fulfill their inner aspirations. While money, fame, or recognition may have some importance, these individuals prioritize making a meaningful impact in their lives, families, communities, or workplaces. Whether through fostering connection, learning new skills, uplifting others, or overcoming challenges, their motivation stems from within, enabling them to set and achieve goals without relying on external validation.

Women are often driven by intrinsic goals, such as creating positive change or uplifting others, rather than external rewards. This internal drive helps us navigate setbacks with resilience and perseverance.

We get a clearer sense of purpose when we get to know ourselves and our values (remember self-reflection in Chapter 2). It serves as a powerful source of motivation by giving our actions meaning and direction. When we are clear on our purpose, we are fueled by a deeper sense of why we do what we do, which helps us stay focused and resilient, even in the face of challenges. We live with intention and see that our lives have meaning. Purpose ignites passion and fosters commitment, reminding us of the impact we aim to create and the goals we strive to achieve. It transforms effort into fulfillment and the inspiration to follow our dreams.

For many years, I've had the privilege of working with an extraordinary woman in Kenya named Violet, whose deep commitment to her community and steadfast values have transformed countless lives. Originally, her work focused on organizing farming and food production for a horticultural company. However, Violet couldn't ignore the heartbreaking reality that many women and babies in her community were dying during childbirth due to a lack of care and facilities. The nearest hospital was far away, and even for those who could reach it, the cost of giving birth there was often unaffordable.

One pivotal moment came when Violet witnessed a woman being rushed to the hospital in a wheelbarrow. The journey was too long, and the woman was forced to deliver her baby without trained medical care. Although informal groups of "traditional birth assistants"—akin to early midwives—offered some help, they lacked the necessary facilities and resources, and tragedies were far too common. Violet, deeply moved by her values of care and justice for women, decided that this situation was unacceptable and set out to find solutions.

She enlisted the help of her father-in-law, a retired doctor and church leader, and together they began building a support system for pregnant women. She convinced the nearest hospital to train the traditional birth assistants, organized a pre- and post-natal clinic within the local church, and eventually secured funding for an ambulance to serve the community. These efforts culminated in the founding of the Shibuye Community Health Workers in 1999, a group created by and for grassroots women to meet their community's pressing health needs.

Violet's ability to see the challenges around her and take decisive action reflects her unwavering dedication to justice and care. Her purpose-driven leadership and courage to step up, speak out, and organize has not only improved the lives of countless women but also turned a shared dream into a lasting legacy of hope and empowerment for her community.

Empathy

Another pillar of emotional intelligence that we have visited is empathy. As described in previous pages, empathy and EQ are intimately intertwined. Emotional intelligence involves recognizing, interpreting, and managing emotions—both our own and those of others—and empathy provides the insight needed to grasp the feelings and perspectives of those around us. Without empathy, the ability to respond to the feelings of others, build strong relationships, and navigate social situations effectively would be significantly diminished, creating a void in EQ. Together, EQ and empathy create a foundation for bonding and increased understanding, trust, and collaboration.

Empathy strengthens collaboration, trust, and team dynamics. It's about seeing the world through others' eyes and addressing their needs compassionately. Women's natural inclination toward empathy often enables them to anticipate challenges, diffuse conflicts, and foster inclusivity.

During the COVID-19 pandemic, I was teaching Women and Gender Studies at a Texas university when students were abruptly sent home to study under challenging circumstances. One of my honors students faced particular difficulty when her family merged households, leaving six children to share just two computers for online schooling. Her personal computer became communal, forcing her to study late into the night. She considered dropping out due to the sheer exhaustion of supporting the merged households, child care, and her studies.

Determined to help, I contacted student affairs, but the initial option to rent a computer was declined by her family due to financial concerns. What if the computer broke, how could they afford a replacement? Refusing to give up, I connected with someone who truly understood her struggles. Through empathy and action, this woman secured a computer for my student, providing the lifeline she needed . That single act of compassion from this woman, who knew neither me nor my student, gave that student the resources she needed to endure the pandemic and ultimately thrive.

Social Skills

As discussed in Chapter 1, these interpersonal skills used to be considered soft skills. But in the new leadership paradigm, they are in demand and essential to your ability to align people towards a common goal. Networking, resolving conflicts, and fostering collaboration are key areas where women excel, often creating inclusive environments where everyone feels valued. Their ability to communicate effectively and build relationships often leads to strong, cohesive teams. They encompass the ability to communicate clearly, actively listen, resolve conflicts, and foster trust—all essential for connection and inclusivity. Other social skills include patience, flexibility, and reliability. And I think that society has broadcast the message that these are qualities a woman should possess.

When your partner has to cancel plans for dinner and drinks because of work, do you feel angry or frustrated? For 25 years, I was married to a surgeon who often had to respond to emergencies. Sometimes I would show up at "couples" parties alone. Other people in medical relationships understood. But, on many occasions, people unfamiliar with the lifestyle would ask me how I could tolerate this behavior. Understanding and flexibility. My expectations of our relationship included an understanding of his commitment to his patients.

How do you react when someone at work struggles to meet a deadline? Effective social skills can resolve the issue while maintaining trust. **Empathy** helps you understand their challenges, while **active listening** shows you value their perspective. Use **clear communication** to address the impact constructively and focus on solutions through **collaboration**. Employ **conflict resolution** if tensions arise and demonstrate **adaptability** by adjusting plans if needed. These skills foster accountability and strengthen team relationships.

In contrast, a young manager I know was extremely rigid about deadlines, viewing them as the ultimate measure of reliability and judging colleagues accordingly. However, when her own circumstances caused her to miss deadlines, she gave herself flexibility without questioning her reliability. This double standard strained team relationships, ultimately alienating her direct reports, with some leaving for other opportunities.

Women leaders excel in prioritizing collaboration, empathy, and building trust, fostering inclusive environments where diverse voices are valued, and ideas flow freely. Through open communication, active listening, and mutual respect, they strengthen teams and navigate challenges with sensitivity and insight. This relational approach requires emotional intelligence and drives innovation, inspires loyalty, and creates a lasting impact, transforming workplaces into supportive, high-performing spaces.

Practical steps you can take to enhance your emotional intelligence in these five areas include:

- **Self-awareness:** Reflect on your emotions and triggers. Challenge your inner critic, as my friend Pat does by telling "Charlie" to "shut up."

- **Self-regulation:** Mindfulness and meditation enhance emotional intelligence by helping leaders stay grounded, reduce stress, and connect with their inner selves. Even a brief daily practice, like ten minutes of mindful breathing, can improve focus and emotional regulation.

- **Motivation:** Align your actions with your values and purpose. That's also called integrity.

- **Empathy:** Listen actively and practice curiosity to understand others' perspectives.

- **Social skills:** Prioritize open communication and collaboration to build trust.

Overcoming Challenges and Bias with Emotional Intelligence

Women leaders face unique challenges because of social expectations of their roles and behaviors. Emotional intelligence equips women to navigate these complexities.

Balancing Empathy and Authority

One such challenge women leaders often navigate is the "double bind," which requires them to balance empathy with assertiveness in ways that male leaders are less frequently expected to. On one hand, they are often encouraged to lead with empathy—listening, nurturing, and prioritizing relationships. These qualities are traditionally associated with femininity and can make them appear more approachable and relatable. However, if they lean too far into empathy, they risk being perceived as weak, overly accommodating, or lacking authority.

On the other hand, when women leaders display assertiveness—speaking directly, setting firm boundaries, or making tough decisions—they can be unfairly judged as aggressive, unlikable, or "too much." This bias creates a narrow margin for women to lead effectively without being criticized for not fitting societal expectations.

This double bind forces women leaders to navigate a constant balancing act, adjusting their leadership style depending on the context while ensuring their decisions are respected and their teams feel valued. Mastering this balance requires emotional intelligence, self-awareness, and resilience to push back against these biases while remaining authentic to their leadership style.

Avoid empathy overload by setting clear boundaries. Lead with compassion while maintaining clarity in decision-making to ensure you're respected and effective.

Reframing Vulnerability

As leadership styles that emphasized stoicism lost their appeal after the pandemic, authentic leadership rose to prominence. Embracing vulnerability and acknowledging weaknesses became recognized as a strength, ushering in the era of vulnerable leadership.

According to Brené Brown, "Giving feedback, receiving feedback, problem solving, ethical decision-making... These are all born of vulnerability." She also asserts that,

"No vulnerability, no creativity. No tolerance for failure, no innovation."

Brené Brown has spent more than two decades researching and sharing her stories about courage, vulnerability, shame, and empathy, and is the author of six number-one New York Times bestselling books.

Vulnerability presents unique challenges for women, as it has long been stereotyped as a sign of feminine weakness, excessive emotionality, or hormonal instability. The act of openly sharing emotions or struggles is often misinterpreted as powerlessness or helplessness. Furthermore, societal perceptions of vulnerability are influenced by intersecting identities such as race, gender, sexual orientation, socioeconomic background, age, or cultural heritage.

For instance, a woman from a marginalized group may face stereotypes that frame her vulnerability as a lack of competence or strength, while a woman from a more privileged background might be perceived as relatable or courageous for expressing similar emotions. These biases illustrate how intersecting identities shape the interpretation and judgment of vulnerability, often placing additional hurdles in the path of women leaders striving to balance authenticity and resilience.

Serena Williams, probably the greatest tennis player of all time, has often shared her vulnerability. After almost dying from complications after the birth of her daughter, she worried about her future. "There's no escaping the fear," she says in the HBO series Being Serena. "The fear that I might not come back as strong as I was. The fear that I can't be both the best mother and the best tennis player in the world." Although applauded by most for vulnerability, she still endured the same racial slurs and body shaming which has accompanied her whole career. Others steeped their response in the "Strong Black Woman" stereotype that assumes Black women should be unbreakable and stoic, especially as a successful athlete. This double standard can make it more challenging for women from marginalized groups to navigate leadership with authenticity.

Such biased misinterpretations can overshadow the strength it takes to be vulnerable, especially when it's framed as a courageous step toward connection, authenticity, and growth.

Women excel at many skills related to EQ. We are usually good at reading subtle social cues, understanding interpersonal dynamics, and demonstrating key emotional intelligence skills such as emotional awareness, adaptability, curiosity, and honest communication. These abilities enable us to build trust, foster collaboration, and effectively manage diverse teams while navigating the complexities of modern leadership. A Korn Ferry study of 55,000 professionals across 90 countries found that women outperformed men in 11 of 12 key areas of emotional and social intelligence, underscoring their leadership strengths.

Exceptional Judgement of Character

Women are often adept at reading unspoken communication, understanding context, and navigating complex interpersonal dynamics. As already discussed, they notice subtle cues like body language, intonation in speech, facial expressions, eye contact, etc. that contribute to the evaluation of people they meet. My friend Sunnie never ceases to amaze me with her incredible ability to assess people. She's interacted with so many different individuals through a wide range of life experiences, and it shows. In her leadership roles, she has this remarkable talent for recognizing someone's strengths and matching them perfectly with roles or opportunities that bring out their best. This "people sense" allows her to manage diverse teams effectively.

Curiosity

Women leaders who genuinely embrace curiosity foster workplaces where relationships and innovation thrive. By showing interest in team members' experiences, stories, and challenges, they create an environment where diverse perspectives are valued. Curiosity goes beyond asking questions; it's about listening attentively, building trust, and inspiring collaboration and creativity. When people feel safe to share their ideas, even unconventional ones, it opens the door to innovative solutions.

For example, a woman noticing a colleague struggling with a project might ask, "What part of the project is hardest for you?" or "What do you think would make this easier?" By genuinely seeking her colleague's perspective, she encourages problem solving, self-expression, and confidence while fostering a sense of being understood.

Curiosity has a ripple effect. When leaders model it, their teams adopt the same mindset, transforming the workplace into a dynamic environment where ideas flourish. This cultural shift leverages diversity as a competitive advantage, resulting in inclusive, creative, and effective solutions.

For women leaders, curiosity is more than a personal trait—it's a tool to strengthen connections, empower teams, and spark innovation, driving lasting success by unlocking the full potential of their organizations.

Relationship Building

Many women naturally prioritize relationship-building, recognizing it as key to effective leadership. By mentoring peers, connecting with clients, or fostering collaboration, they create environments where individuals feel valued and understood. This focus on empathy and communication aligns with their strengths, helping to build trust, boost morale, and drive collective success.

Women leaders' relational approach strengthens team dynamics and empowers others to contribute their best. In a world that increasingly values authenticity and connection, their ability to lead through relationships positions them as transformative and impactful leaders.

Honest Communication

Women leaders who communicate directly but compassionately strike a balance between authenticity and advocacy, ensuring their voices are heard while respecting others. Honest communication depends on emotional intelligence to balance transparency with sensitivity, ensuring that interactions are respectful, clear, and meaningful.

Adaptability

As you will read in Chapter 7, women often demonstrate an incredible capacity for adapting to change. Since we fulfill so many different roles that often require flexibility, we have learned to navigate shifting priorities and external pressures with agility. This adaptability positions us as steady leaders in times of uncertainty.

Empathy and Emotional Intelligence are essential to the new paradigm of leadership. As women excel in these qualities, they are equipped to lead effectively and compassionately. They are essential for:

Breaking Barriers:

Empathy helps women build coalitions and inspire trust, making it easier to challenge systemic barriers. By understanding the unique struggles of individuals and groups, women leaders can connect with diverse stakeholders, fostering unity and collaboration in their efforts to dismantle inequities and create lasting change.

Fostering Inclusion:

EQ empowers women to create workplaces where diverse voices are heard and valued. By using empathy to understand different perspectives and leveraging social skills to encourage collaboration, women leaders ensure that everyone feels included, respected, and empowered to contribute their best ideas.

Leading Through Complexity:

High EQ equips women to manage the emotional and interpersonal complexities of leadership, turning challenges into opportunities. With the ability to regulate emotions, navigate conflicts, and make thoughtful decisions, women leaders can maintain balance under pressure and guide their teams with clarity and resilience.

I've worked with women who emerged as leaders because of survival. Their abilities and capacity have been tested to the limit. Our work together is not only powered by a shared vision, but also by shared vulnerabilities and the trust built through knowing exactly who they are, what they value, and where they stand. Their adversities forced them to recognize their existing strengths and gaps and motivated them to explore alternative strategies for growth and to accomplish their goals.

Such adaptation mechanisms prompted one woman to create a group to support women farmers. Frustrated that women were traditionally doing the work in the field to cultivate and produce crops, but the money was going to the land owners, she organized women to pool their money and buy some land of their own. As their crops flourished and they were being paid for their work, they bought more land. This cooperative now owns thousands of acres and provides livelihoods for 10,000 families. She knew she was an expert in horticulture, but wasn't as strong in relationship building. She led her cause by engaging other women with those skills to join her.

Actionable Steps for Developing EQ:

- Practice mindfulness to stay present and grounded.
- Engage in self-reflection to deepen self-awareness.
- Set boundaries to protect your emotional energy.
- Cultivate curiosity to build stronger connections.
- Seek mentorship and role models to learn and grow.

Empathy and emotional intelligence are not just tools for leadership—they're transformative leadership strengths and catalysts for change. Women's ability to lead with emotional intelligence redefines leadership, creating more innovative, and connected spaces. By cultivating self-awareness, empathy, and adaptability, aspiring women leaders can navigate challenges, foster meaningful connections, and lead with authenticity.

Leadership begins with knowing yourself—your values, strengths, and purpose—and showing up authentically. Through self-reflection and intentional growth, you can harness these strengths to create lasting impact and drive positive change.

If you haven't yet, get your free downloadable companion Workbook at cathyholt.com/unstoppableworkbook to go deeper on the chapter, write down your thoughts, and consider these takeaways and action steps.

Chapter 4

Communication

As discussed in Chapter 1, leadership is not merely defined by a title or position; it transcends formal roles and power structures. At its core, leadership is the capacity to inspire, guide, and influence others in pursuit of a shared vision or common objective. It is less about authority and more about the ability to create an environment where people feel motivated and supported to contribute their best, driving success and growth for the group as a whole. Communication is essential for effective leadership, shaping how leaders inspire, influence, and build strong connections with others. It plays a crucial role in fostering trust, aligning efforts, and motivating people or teams to achieve shared goals. The most effective leaders are strong communicators who excel at expressing themselves both verbally and in writing. They can adapt their communication style to connect with people from diverse backgrounds, roles, levels, and locations.

For women leaders, communication is both a powerful tool and a complex challenge, as societal expectations and gender norms often shape perceptions of our messaging and delivery. This chapter delves into the intricate relationship between women leaders and communication, exploring how they navigate unique hurdles while leveraging their strengths to nurture connection, equity, and empowerment. By examining real-world examples, practical strategies, and the broader cultural landscape, this chapter aims to show women leaders how to harness the power of communication to lead authentically and effectively in diverse environments.

The Role of Communication in Leadership

Effective communication lies at the heart of successful leadership, serving as the bridge between vision and action. Leaders use communication to articulate goals, share visions, and inspire others to follow. Through clear, consistent, and authentic communication, leaders build trust, foster collaboration, and navigate challenges. Whether rallying a team in the face of adversity or celebrating collective successes, strong communication skills enable leaders to connect with others and drive meaningful change.

Communication is not a solo performance; it's a dialogue. While discussions on leadership often emphasize the importance of shaping a message for the audience, the concept can feel abstract. What does it truly mean to tailor communication? It means recognizing that words hold power, and their impact depends on their resonance and clarity for the audience. Knowing who you're addressing and using language they can relate to is crucial. For example, the way you explain where babies come from to a young child would naturally differ from how you present the topic in a high school reproductive health class. The key is ensuring your audience can grasp the language and concepts you use.

This principle becomes especially evident in everyday scenarios. Take technology for example. While I enjoy using it, I find myself frustrated when something goes wrong and tech support overwhelms me with jargon. Their explanation might be precise, but if I don't understand it, are they truly communicating? In those moments, I often ask them to explain as if I were a child—

though many children are more tech-savvy than I am! When we don't use words our audience can relate to, the conversation becomes one-sided, an information dump devoid of understanding.

Effective communication, particularly in leadership, is multidimensional. It involves words, emotions, listening, and an awareness of the audience's state of mind. It means actively engaging with your audience, ensuring your message resonates with their knowledge, perspective, and needs. True communication happens only when your message is not just delivered but understood.

This requires a deep understanding of your audience so you can share information in a way that invites engagement. It's not just about the words you choose but also the tone and style you use to deliver them. As a communicator, it's partly your responsibility to adapt your message to ensure it connects. A classic example of poor adaptation is speaking English to someone whose first language isn't English. Instead of simplifying or clarifying, some might raise their voice or slow down, assuming it aids comprehension—but it doesn't. True communication is about meeting people where they are, not simply repeating yourself louder or slower.

Strategies often cited to communicate effectively include:

Be clear and concise

As we just read, words and knowing your audience matters. In addition, it is important to know what you are truly trying to convey. Clear and concise communication isn't about oversimplifying—it's about delivering your message in a way that's easy to understand, ensuring your audience knows exactly what you're getting at. Too much information or unnecessary background detracts from the main point of the conversation. I call this going off on a tangent. We've all encountered someone who shares TMI (too much information) during a discussion. You know you have to set aside 30 minutes of conversation time to get an answer to a simple question. Instead of providing clarity about their message, their extra details can make it harder for us to focus on their main points. Personally, I find that when someone overloads a conversation with information not on topic, I get so distracted trying to process it all that I lose track of the original purpose of the discussion.

As a leader, learning how to get a conversation back on track is a great skill. Actively listening to discern if the extra information actually adds to their point is key. If it does, you can say something like "thanks for that perspective, how do you think that adds to our conversation about …" If it doesn't, gently reminding them of the topic is in order. Phrases that can be helpful in refocusing a conversation might include: "Thank you for sharing that, but I'd like to continue focusing on …" or more directly, "How does this relate to our original topic of …?

Keeping the message clear and to the point helps ensure that everyone stays aligned on the main topic or goal of the conversation, avoiding unnecessary confusion or distraction.

Be aware of your non-verbal communications

Communication experts say that about 90% of communication involves cues such as facial expressions, body language, eye contact, and tone of voice. Aligning how you present yourself with the words you are speaking is key to communicating effectively.

Even when we aren't speaking, our wordless communication often broadcasts our true feelings. When we ask someone how they are doing and they say, "Fine!" but their arms are crossed, their frown lines are creased, and they won't make eye contact, we know everything is far from fine. That response and the contrasting body language can result in confusion and tension, potentially leading to distrust.

In contrast, when your words and nonverbal signals are in sync, you strengthen understanding, credibility, and rapport. Just like emotional intelligence (Chapter 3), awareness is key to aligning your nonverbal cues with your spoken words.

Pay attention to your body language when communicating with others. Are you distracted, crossing your arms, hunched over, fidgeting, or checking your phone? These actions often reflect negative emotions like disinterest or discomfort, which can undermine your words. Conversely, making eye contact, leaning in, or smiling signals interest and connection. Notice how you react when others display these behaviors with you.

Awareness of your physical cues is the first step to managing nonverbal communication. Practice positive body language to complement your verbal skills. For deeper insight, ask a trusted friend or colleague to observe you in action and provide feedback. Treat their input as a gift and incorporate it into your actions to show you value their perspective. Ignoring feedback can erode trust, but applying it fosters growth and engagement as a leader.

When I was working in politics, I had the good fortune of training with a communications consultant. I am a bit taller than average, well-spoken, and a bit on the assertive side. She pointed out that I could be intimidating when I speak. One tactic she taught me to connect more effectively with state legislators (mostly male) was to sit when I was talking to them. Just that act, combined with using body language that invited conversation, helped us have better dialogues. I also learned that when I really wanted to make a point or assert my legitimacy, I would stand up to speak. I adapted my nonverbal language to different situations to reach my goals.

Non-verbal communication can vary greatly in different cultures and communities. Awareness and observation of people in conversations can provide you clues to differences in positive body language. For example, direct eye contact in our Western culture signals interest, whereas lowering your eyes is considered polite in Asian cultures. In some Middle Eastern cultures, direct eye contact between people of the opposite sex is considered inappropriate. The concept of personal space and the physical distance maintained during conversations varies across cultures. Shaking hands is popular in some cultures and avoided in others. If you are going to lead internationally, knowing nonverbal cultural norms is essential to productive communication and inspiring and motivating others around your passion.

Engage in active listening

This skill from Chapter 1 just keeps popping up —probably because it's so important. As a quick recap when we listen actively, we are listening to learn. We pay attention to words, feelings, and nonverbal cues in our effort to understand someone's perspective. Much of our conditioning revolves around listening with the intent to respond. In school, we were often taught the art of debate—how to communicate persuasively and defend our ideas. While this is a valuable skill in certain situations, it often gets in the way of truly listening to understand or learn from another person's perspective. Instead of being open to new insights, we focus on crafting a rebuttal, which can limit opportunities for growth, empathy, and deeper connections.

According to communication expert and professor at Harvard University's Management Department, Marjorie North, most of us only remember about half of what we hear even when we think we're really paying attention. Since listening is a crucial leadership skill, we need to amp up our ability to hear and retain information from conversations, i.e. listen attentively. Professor North suggests three strategies to improve our listening.

1. Set aside any preconceived notions you may have about the speaker's appearance or past behavior.

2. Clear your mind by fully concentrating on their words rather than planning your reply.

3. Show interest and encourage them to share more by asking open-ended questions and using supportive gestures, such as nodding.

I know I have caught myself on many occasions thinking, "I already know what you are going to say." Now I try and ask myself, "What is this person really telling me?"

Enhance your emotional intelligence

Here I am again, writing about EQ (Chapter 3). But once again, I need to emphasize that this ability is key to impactful communication and leadership.

As discussed in Chapter 3, self-awareness is the foundation of emotional intelligence. To communicate effectively, you must first understand yourself—your values, emotional triggers, biases, and mental wellness.

Margaret Andrews, a professor at Harvard, reinforces this in her article *How to Improve Your Emotional Intelligence*: "If you're aware of your own emotions and the behaviors they trigger, you can begin to manage these emotions and behaviors."

Regulating your emotions creates space to respond thoughtfully rather than reacting impulsively, fostering meaningful and productive conversations. For instance, imagine a colleague openly criticizes your work in a meeting. Your initial reaction might be defensive, saying, *"That's unfair, and you don't even understand the context!"* Such a response could escalate tension. Instead, by pausing, breathing, and collecting your thoughts, you could respond calmly: *"I appreciate your feedback. Can you help me understand your concerns in more detail so we can address them together?"* This approach diffuses tension, promotes problem solving, and fosters professionalism.

Leaders with strong emotional intelligence excel at active listening, maintaining a calm tone, and using positive body language to convey openness and respect. Emotional intelligence isn't solely about managing your own emotions; it's also about understanding and empathizing with others. Empathy enhances communication by allowing you to genuinely connect and acknowledge others' feelings and perspectives.

When people feel heard and valued, they engage in more honest, productive discussions. Empathy also helps navigate tough conversations, easing tension and transforming potential conflict into meaningful dialogue. Women often excel at tuning into others' experiences and tailoring messages to resonate. This ability strengthens relationships and creates a foundation for authentic and impactful communication.

Communicate to connect

As I have said, an important goal of communicating is connection. By being clear, engaging, and expressive and using your voice and facial expressions to bring energy to your message, you are more likely to build rapport, establish bonds, bridge gaps, build trust, and strengthen relationships.

Keep in mind that communication is dynamic. Preparing in advance by knowing what you are trying to communicate, understanding your audience, and paying attention to your nonverbal cues will help you develop understanding though dialogue. But it's equally important to stay attuned to your audience during the interaction. As one friend of mine puts it, she is constantly taking the temperature of the room. She is noticing if the people she is talking with are getting restless, seem bored or confused or if they are leaning in and engaged. Depending on her observations, she adjusts her approach. She might add humor, ask questions, or change her approach and language. Sticking rigidly to a communication style can create roadblocks to understanding and connecting. By being flexible and responsive to your communication partners, you are more likely to build trust and come together in common understanding and purpose.

Storytelling is a powerful communication strategy for women, allowing them to convey ideas and values in a relatable and memorable way. By sharing personal experiences or narratives, women can connect emotionally with their audience, making their message more impactful and inspiring. Storytelling also helps to break down complex concepts into accessible and engaging content, fostering understanding and collaboration. For women leaders, storytelling is not just a tool for communication but a way to build trust, influence perspectives, and inspire action while staying authentic to their voice.

Stories have a remarkable impact on how information is remembered and understood. Research shows that stories are up to 22 times more memorable than facts alone and can increase conversion rates by 30%. Additionally, people retain only 5% to 10% of material when it's presented as statistics, but they remember 65% to 70% when the information is shared through a story. This demonstrates the power of storytelling as an effective communication tool for making messages resonate and stick.

There are strategies to the art of impactful storytelling. A primary one is knowing the core message you are trying to convey. Once again, you have to know your audience so you can craft your story with situations they can relate to.

In one developing country, a group of women were struggling to convince their community leaders to cut down the tall weeds along a road they used to get to the bus and work. The women explained that they were being dragged into the bushes and assaulted, but this alarming reality failed to prompt action from the male leaders. They reframed their message by focusing on the economic impact of their fear and the assaults. They shared stories about how missing work was affecting their ability to earn money needed for food, necessities, and supporting their families. They showed how this, in turn, hurt the productivity of local employers and the community's economy. Using this perspective, they connected with the leaders—it made them care. As a result, the weeds were cut down, creating a safer environment for everyone.

Your story must also be concise. Build your compelling narrative around the message you want to communicate and how you want them to react and respond. Just like any other communications, you need to get to and make your point without rambling and "going off on a tangent."

As Leslie Capps, The Strategic Storypreneur and author of *Turn Your Story Into Business Gold* writes, "Your story is your leadership signature—it's how people know what you stand for and why it matters. A well-told story builds trust, creates connection, and inspires action. Great leaders don't just tell stories; they use them to help others shape their future."

For women leaders, communication plays an even more critical role, as they often face unique challenges such as overcoming gender biases or navigating perceptions around assertiveness. Despite these hurdles, many renowned women leaders have demonstrated exceptional communication skills that have set them apart and amplified their impact.

Take, for instance, **Jacinda Ardern**, the former Prime Minister of New Zealand. Her empathetic and transparent communication style during crises, such as the Christchurch terrorist attacks and the COVID-19 pandemic, earned her widespread respect and admiration. By connecting on a human level and providing clear, actionable information, she demonstrated how effective communication can strengthen leadership.

Another example is **Michelle Obama**, whose ability to weave storytelling into her speeches has inspired millions. Through her powerful narratives and relatable tone, she not only advocated for issues like education and health but also connected with people on a deeply personal level. Her communication style exemplifies how authenticity and emotional resonance can elevate a leader's message.

These examples highlight that successful leadership is not just about what is communicated but how it is communicated. Women leaders who master the art of engaging, transparent, and values-driven communication can overcome barriers, inspire trust, and create lasting impact in their organizations and beyond.

Gender and Communication Styles

Gender bias plays a big role in how women's communication is judged, creating unique challenges for women leaders as they navigate expectations around leadership. Let's explore some of the gender differences in communication styles.

How Women and Men Are Often Socialized to Communicate

How we're taught to communicate starts at an early age and shapes how we express ourselves. Girls are often encouraged to be nice, to share, to listen, and to avoid conflict. We're taught to nurture others and focus on relationships and how others feel.

Boys, on the other hand, are more likely to be pushed to be assertive, competitive, goal driven, and to take risks. This encouraged behavior often translates into more direct and dominant communication styles. These differences don't just vanish as we grow—they influence how we express ourselves in personal, professional, and, eventually, even leadership roles.

For example, women may lean towards using more collaborative and inclusive language that may downplay their accomplishments to maintain harmony. Men may adopt more direct, assertive, and competitive tones to establish authority. Neither is better or worse, but these differences can lead to misunderstandings in mixed-gender communication, especially in leadership where communication styles are under the spotlight. These misunderstandings can also lead to biases in the perceptions of leadership capabilities.

How Society Shapes Women's Communication in Leadership

Overcoming Biases and Stereotypes

One of the toughest hurdles women face in leadership is the double bind: if a woman is assertive, she risks being labeled as "too aggressive" or "not feminine enough." On the other hand, if she adopts a more collaborative or empathetic style, she may be perceived as weak or lacking authority. This creates a difficult dilemma, forcing women to carefully balance strength and approachability in ways their male counterparts rarely have to consider. Assertiveness, which is typically admired in men, is often scrutinized in women, leading to unfair judgments about their competence or temperament. At the same time, displaying empathy or collaboration—qualities frequently associated with women—can result in being underestimated as a leader. This double bind doesn't just limit women's opportunities; it adds mental and emotional strain as they navigate these conflicting expectations, striving to find a leadership style that is both effective and authentic.

And that's why it gets tricky: as women leaders, societal expectations can make us feel like we're walking on a tightrope. On one hand, we're expected to exhibit traditional "feminine" traits such as being approachable, warm, and empathetic because that's what society often associates with women. On the other hand, leadership also demands those "masculine" traits of confidence, decisiveness, and authority.

This double standard puts women in a double bind. If we stray too far in either direction, we risk being judged and often criticized. Be too assertive, and people might label you as aggressive a refer to you as that B word. Be too warm, collaborative, or empathetic and they might see you as "too soft" and weak. Does this sound familiar to anyone else? It definitely hits home for me.

Another layer of bias stems from the stereotype that women are more emotional or sensitive than men. This stereotype is one of the most deeply rooted gender stereotypes in the Western world. Both men and women associate "emotion" with femininity even though anger is an emotion and typically more masculine. Often times, people have these perceived rules about what and when emotions can be displayed. Men don't cry; men can show anger, but angry women are erratic and irrational.

In 2014, Jill Abramson, the first female executive editor of *The New York Times*, was abruptly dismissed from her role. Reports suggested that her management style was perceived as "pushy" and "difficult," terms often used to critique assertive women. Critics noted that similar behavior in male leaders—standing firm, demanding accountability, and pushing for excellence— would typically be viewed as strong leadership. Her dismissal sparked widespread discussion about the double standards women face when displaying the same assertiveness or authority as their male counterparts.

This stereotype of women and emotions can lead to their communication being scrutinized more intensely. For example, a passionate argument from a woman leader might be dismissed as overly emotional, while a similar tone from a male leader could be interpreted as passionate and inspiring. This bias can undermine women's authority, even when their communication is well-reasoned and impactful.

Yet a study conducted by the Harvard Business Review of 137 leaders and their subordinates in Europe during COVID-19 showed that women expressed higher levels of anxiety than men about the pandemic. However, despite experiencing higher levels of anxiety, women were less likely than men to allow their emotions to negatively affect their leadership.

The new paradigm of leadership that acknowledges the importance of emotional intelligence is slowly reframing the role of emotions in leading effectively. Emotions exist in any circumstance. It is how we understand and manage them that matters.

These biases and social expectations can make it hard to feel like you're showing up authentically. It's not just about what you say—it's about how you say it, how you carry yourself, and even how others perceive your tone. These double standards are exhausting, but they also present an opportunity for you to carve out your own authentic style of communication that blends strength with connection and authority with empathy.

Navigating Conflict

As you read in Chapter 3, women often excel in emotional intelligence, a key leadership quality that encompasses self-awareness, empathy, and the ability to manage emotions effectively. This capability enables women to navigate conflict with a balance of understanding and composure. By recognizing their own emotional triggers, women can approach tense situations thoughtfully rather than reactively. Their natural empathy allows them to see conflicts from multiple perspectives. Acknowledging how each person's many identities affect their journeys through life and their views of the world serves as a basis for conversations across differences. Women often look beyond these differences and focus on commonalities and what is shared. This plays a crucial role in fostering relationships and building connections between people. Such connections spark curiosity about diverse perspectives and encourage open-mindedness. Additionally, strong emotional intelligence helps women build trust, facilitating open and constructive dialogue to de-escalate tension and foster mutual understanding even in challenging conversations.

These strengths not only support resolving conflicts effectively but also create an environment where collaboration and respect can thrive.

Digital and Virtual Communication

At this point, I'd like to include a few observations about digital and virtual communication. The pandemic showed us that virtual meetings can work. In fact, a study in the Harvard Business Review showed that employees participated in 60% more virtual meetings in 2022 compared to 2020. I know I also communicate more with friends and family across distances through various modes of video chatting. Given this new reality, I wanted to see if there were gender differences in communicating in the digital world. And there are.

Women face some of the same challenges of communicating in virtual meetings as they do in person. Men tend to take up more of the airtime, and women are more likely to be interrupted. Some strategies to consider include:

- Establish clear guidelines before the meeting, such as using the "raise hand" feature to signal when someone wants to speak.

- Assign a moderator to oversee the flow of the meeting and ensure everyone has a chance to contribute.

- Create a system for turn-taking to keep the discussion organized and respectful.

- Clearly communicate the agenda and objectives at the start to keep the meeting focused.

- If interrupted, politely but firmly reassert your point with phrases like, " *I would like to finish my thought,*" while staying calm and composed.

- Anticipate potential disruptions by promoting active listening, addressing dominant speakers constructively, and fostering a balanced and inclusive discussion.

Because of our emotional intelligence, we tend to read the room and look more for nonverbal communication when interacting. This is made more difficult when you can only see someone's face on the "Hollywood Squares" type lineup on the screen. You can still watch for facial cues and also tune into tone and word choices through active listening that will provide insight into more subtle messaging. If you recognize someone needs encouragement or needs to express themselves more fully, you can suggest that you meet separately online.

Adapting communication skills for digital platforms is essential for women leaders in today's interconnected world. Virtual meetings, social media, and digital forums require clear, concise messaging, active engagement, and an understanding of platform-specific etiquette. However, women leaders often face unique challenges online, especially on social media platforms, including gendered harassment, trolling, and scrutiny of their appearance or tone. To navigate these issues, women can use tools like privacy settings, blocking, and reporting features, while leaning on supportive networks and allies for encouragement. Despite these challenges, digital platforms offer powerful opportunities to build a personal brand. By sharing authentic stories, demonstrating expertise, and engaging thoughtfully with audiences, women leaders can establish a strong and credible presence online, amplifying their voice and influence.

Strategies to Adapt and Thrive in Communicating Like Leaders

You don't need to conform to one extreme communication style or the other. Navigating these stereotypes requires a balance of self-awareness, adaptability, and authenticity. Great leaders develop effective communication strategies to navigate and succeed in diverse environments and with a variety of audiences. You can find your authentic style and stay true to yourself. Here are some strategies women leaders can use to overcome biases without compromising who they are:

a. **Find Your Balance:**
Women often adopt a communication style that combines empathy and assertiveness. They command respect without alienating others by using inclusive language and listening actively. You can balance warmth with authority while confidently sharing your vision. For example, using phrases like *"Here's what I believe will work, and I'd love to hear your thoughts"* shows both confidence and collaboration.

b. **Leverage Emotional Intelligence:**
Emotional intelligence is one of your biggest superpowers. As I wrote earlier in this chapter and in Chapter 3, EQ helps you read the room, manage your emotions, and respond thoughtfully to others. Using emotional intelligence when communicating with diverse groups fosters trust and collaboration. It's especially helpful in tough conversations, conflict resolution, or when dealing with team dynamics.

c. **Tailor Your Message:**
Every audience is different, so adapt your communication to fit. Adjusting your tone, vocabulary, or style can help the message resonate better with each different group. In a boardroom, you might focus on data and results. Supporting your point of view with facts and data can shift the focus from personal delivery to the substance of the message. When talking with your team, partners or collaborators, you might emphasize the "why" behind decisions to make them feel more included. You can inspire them by focusing on values and impact.

d. **Reframe Assertiveness:**
Being assertive doesn't mean being harsh. To address biases, many women leaders practice techniques to assert themselves with clarity and confidence without being perceived negatively. Using inclusive language like "we" and "our" can help make statements appear more team-focused and collaborative rather than overly authoritative.

This also might include framing their ideas as questions or solutions rather than demands. For example, instead of saying *"I think we should..."* try *"I believe this is the best approach because..."* Direct language backed up by facts or experiences projects authority without alienating others.

e. **Support and Amplify:**
   Women often create support networks by mentoring or sponsoring other women. Sharing knowledge or opportunities for advancement provides a foundation for women's voices to be heard. One of the best things we can do as women leaders is amplify each other. If you're in a meeting and a woman colleague shares a great idea, repeat it and give her credit. For example, *"I love what Sarah said earlier about..."* This helps ensure their voice is heard and respected.

f. **Challenge Bias:**
   Sometimes, you have to address it head on by calmly challenging stereotypes and reframing perceptions. If someone interrupts you or dismisses your idea, calmly bring it back. Try something like, *"Before we move on, I'd like to finish what I was saying."* It's about validating your perspective without escalating the situation. This not only helps in individual interactions, but also sets a precedent for shifting cultural norms.

The most important thing to remember is that your voice matters. You are the expert of your life and lived experiences, and that gives you a unique perspective. Your communication style is a reflection of who you are as a leader. By balancing strength and empathy, tailoring your approach to your audience, and standing firm in your values and convictions, you can lead effectively while remaining true to yourself. Whether you're naturally more direct or more empathetic, there's no one "right" way to communicate. Leadership isn't about fitting into someone else's mold—it's about finding your own style and using it to inspire, connect, and lead authentically.

Ultimately, overcoming gender bias requires a combination of individual strategies by women leaders and systemic efforts to address societal norms and workplace cultures that perpetuate inequities. Through resilience, adaptability, and authenticity, many women leaders have successfully challenged these biases, creating space for others to do the same.

If you haven't yet, get your free downloadable companion Workbook at cathyholt.com/unstoppableworkbook to go deeper on the chapter, write down your thoughts, and consider these takeaways and action steps.

Key Takeaways

1. **Communication as Leadership's Foundation**
   a. Leaders inspire, influence, and build trust through clear, authentic communication tailored to diverse audiences.

2. **Multidimensional Communication**
   a. Effective communication involves words, emotions, listening, and nonverbal cues, ensuring messages are both delivered and understood.

3. **Nonverbal and Active Listening**
   a. Body language, tone, and facial expressions impact credibility and trust. Positive cues like eye contact and smiling enhance connection, while active listening fosters understanding and deeper relationships.

4. **Emotional Intelligence**
   a. Self-awareness, emotional regulation, and empathy strengthen communication, helping leaders navigate conflict, connect authentically, and foster trust.

5. **Gender Bias in Communication**
   a. Women leaders face the "double bind": assertiveness may be viewed as aggression, while empathy risks being seen as weakness. Overcoming stereotypes requires balancing strength with warmth.

6. **Practical Strategies**
   a. Adapt messages to audiences, balance authority with empathy, amplify others' voices, and calmly challenge biases to foster inclusivity and collaboration.

7. **Storytelling**
   a. Sharing relatable narratives builds trust, simplifies complex ideas, and inspires action, making messages more memorable and impactful.

8. **Digital and Virtual Communication**
   a. Clear, concise messaging and inclusivity are vital online. Women can navigate challenges like interruptions or scrutiny by using strategies to maintain engagement and amplify their influence.

9. **Thriving Despite Bias**
   a. Women leaders can overcome challenges by blending self-awareness, adaptability, and authenticity, crafting their own leadership communication style.

Chapter 5

Women as Leaders in Creating Collaboration, Team Building, and Trust Building

Significance of Women in Leadership Roles

Over the years, women have gone from being underrepresented in leadership roles to becoming key players in driving change across every field. They've shown a remarkable ability to balance getting results with fostering inclusivity and compassion—creating spaces where collaboration, trust, and teamwork thrive. This shift not only reflects women overcoming long-standing barriers but also shows a growing appreciation for the unique strengths they bring to leadership.

Of course, it hasn't always been easy. Women in leadership have faced their share of systemic challenges, from stereotypes to limited access to decision-making opportunities. But those obstacles have also built resilience, adaptability, and innovation. Today, organizations and communities benefit greatly from the fresh perspectives women bring. Their impact goes beyond boosting the bottom line—they're shaping workplaces and cultures that emphasize equity, connection, and shared success.

Women's personal roles have evolved alongside their professional journeys. How many of you now balance caregiving, partnerships, parenting, and community involvement while striving for professional excellence? These experiences sharpen our ability to juggle responsibilities, demonstrate empathy, and lead with emotional intelligence and strategic vision. As the cornerstone of families and social networks, we often foster collaboration, resolve conflicts, and build trust—skills that enhance our ability to lead authentically and inclusively in every aspect of life.

Why Collaboration, Team Building, and Trust Building Matter

Leadership is more than directing teams or achieving goals—it is about inspiring individuals to collectively contribute their best efforts. At the heart of this process lie three interrelated pillars: collaboration, team building, and trust building. These elements are not just buzzwords but the foundation of sustainable success in any organization or community. Additionally, these three pillars are deeply intertwined with women's lives outside of work, as these skills often form the foundation of healthy relationships, community involvement, and personal growth and fulfillment. Successful women leaders are skilled in these areas, making their contribution particularly vital in today's interconnected and rapidly evolving world. By excelling in collaboration, team building, and trust building, women leaders create spaces where individuals feel valued, inspired, and motivated to achieve collective success. This chapter explores these three pillars and how women uniquely navigate them, and the impact they create through their leadership.

Collaboration is when two or more people work together towards a common goal. It fosters a sense of shared purpose, breaks down silos, and encourages engagement.

Collaboration is also a powerful tool to stimulate creative problem-solving and innovation. When people work together, they are exposed to new skills and diverse points of view. No two people will have the same perspective. We each have unique lived experiences that influence our interactions with the world.

Women are great at fostering collaboration by creating spaces where everyone's voice is heard and diverse perspectives are valued. Drawing on their compassion, creativity, honesty, and willingness to share, they build inclusive environments that can lead to innovative solutions. Additionally, women often participate in activities like volunteering that teach and reinforce the skills of collaboration to achieve shared goals. These activities, as well as friendships, provide guidance and practice at sharing experiences, supporting the needs of others, and navigating group dynamics. Our lives are richer by learning the perspectives of others and working together.

As a university professor, I used this exercise to make the point about considering different perspectives.

I would place a box in the center of the room, carefully arranging the tables into a hollow square so that everyone had a clear view. The box was special—it had different colors and messages on each of its sides. I'd invite everyone to share what they saw. Each description was unique, reflecting the point of view of the person speaking.

Once everyone had spoken, I'd pause and ask them gently, "Now, do you want to argue with anyone about what they see? Or can we agree that we're all describing the same box from our individual perspective?" This was the first step in creating a collaborative classroom environment.

In our personal lives, we often collaborate with partners, children, and extended family members to manage households, plan events, or tackle shared responsibilities. This involves listening, negotiating, and making decisions together to ensure harmony and efficiency. With friends, maintaining meaningful relationships often requires the ability to collaborate on shared experiences, support each other's needs, and navigate group dynamics. Additionally, many women engage with their communities by actively participating in volunteer organizations, neighborhood groups, or school committees, where cooperation is key to achieving shared goals like organizing events or addressing local issues.

Working together and sharing viewpoints can dispel stereotypes as we get to know people from different backgrounds and with different identities. Engaging with people who differ from you can stimulate your brain to break free from habitual thinking patterns and enhance its performance. Studies have shown that groups with diverse perspectives make better decisions by harnessing the collective knowledge and expertise of different individuals.

Cloverpop, a leading decision intelligence platform, reviewed 600 decisions made by 200 different business teams. Their findings showed that diverse teams (gender, age, race, culture, etc.) made better decisions 87% of the time. All male teams came in at 58%, while teams with both men and women were higher at 73%. We brainstorm better in groups! Studies have also shown that collaboration with groups from different backgrounds find solutions more creatively.

Collaboration also helps reach a wider audience as members of the group engage with their networks. What's more, people usually enjoy the social interaction of working together.

As a leader, one of the most impactful ways to foster collaboration is by delegating tasks that align with each group member's strengths. Trying to do it alone is a recipe for burnout and falling short of your goals.

It took a major life wake-up call for me to learn this important lesson. After my daughter's stroke and her father stepping away, I tried to handle everything alone—her rehab, medical issues, appointments, insurance, and her return to college. But I quickly realized I couldn't pour from an empty cup. Asking for help wasn't a weakness; it was self-awareness and self-care. By opening up, I allowed friends who cared deeply about my daughter to share in her recovery. Delegating tasks like transportation, meals, and errands not only lightened my load but also strengthened friendships and showed my daughter the village of support around her.

By effectively delegating, leaders not only share their workload, but also inspire greater commitment to and ownership of the process—participants have a stronger stake in the outcome and are more invested in the project's success.

When people work in areas where they excel, they're more engaged, motivated, and confident, which not only boosts their individual confidence and performance, but also elevates the results. By leveraging everyone's unique talents, you create an environment where contributions are meaningful. Recognizing and utilizing these strengths is key to maximizing the potential of your collaborative efforts. This is where your emotional intelligence and empathy shine. You have gotten to know the people you work with by actively listening to their words, body language, and actions. You used your heightened emotional intelligence and empathy to learn about their perspectives. You've also taken the time to learn about what they are good at and like to do. You use all that intel to delegate activities that provide them with opportunities to succeed,

Delegating a task and delegating an outcome are two different approaches to sharing responsibilities. For example, a mother might ask her teenager to help with dinner by chopping vegetables and setting the table—this is task delegation. The focus is on completing specific actions while she remains responsible for the overall meal. On the other hand, if she asks her teenager to take charge of preparing dinner for the night, with guidance like "Make something easy and balanced," she's delegating an outcome. Here, the teenager is responsible for deciding the menu, cooking the meal, and ensuring it's ready by dinnertime. The difference lies in whether the responsibility is for individual steps or for achieving the overall result.

But delegation doesn't stop there. As we see in the dinner example, when delegating, it's important to clearly set and agree on expectations. Take the time to explain why the task matters and, just as importantly, why the person you're assigning it to is the ideal fit. By painting a clear picture of what success looks like, you empower them and ensure everyone is aligned for a positive outcome.

It is also important to ensure that the person taking on the work has the resources needed to successfully complete their tasks, like the ingredients needed to prepare a dinner. These include access to information, sufficient time, and, when applicable, authority to make certain decisions along the way.

Don't assume everything will fall into place on its own. Stay engaged by checking in periodically to ensure the project stays on track, but without micromanaging. This allows the person responsible to make adjustments if needed before any major issues arise.

Ensure that a debrief is included in the action plan so everyone has the opportunity to learn from the experience.

Another important aspect of collaboration is the power structure. Whether it's due to often being overlooked or ignored in decision-making, or historically having people order us around or control us, many women have a discomfort with power. The very definition of power is the ability to act or produce an effect; possession of control, authority, or influence over others. Based on our lived experiences, we often equate power with aggression, control and subservience. This power over is built on force, coercion, or domination. I don't know about you, but I'm at a stage in my life that if someone tells me I "have to do something," I question why—is this for their benefit or for mine? I don't think I'm alone in that kind of backlash reaction. I know that's how my daughter reacted, and I think still does.

For whatever reason, women tend to share power.

Committing to shared power means making a real, ongoing effort to create a community where everyone, no matter who they are, has what they need to thrive. It's about ensuring people have access to the resources they need, feel valued for who they are and what they contribute, and have a genuine voice in decisions that affect their lives. It also means respecting their autonomy over their own choices and bodies while fostering an environment where they feel both physically and emotionally safe. Shared power isn't just a concept—it's about creating spaces where everyone can truly belong and succeed.

"It's not power over other people; it's the power to do things,"
- Dr. Elsbeth Johnson, MIT Sloan School of Management researcher

Collaborations are enhanced when power is shared. People feel empowered to take ownership of their work and make meaningful contributions. They are more willing to share diverse viewpoints, resulting in more effective problem solving and innovative solutions. And a culture of shared power creates better cohesiveness and fosters teamwork, where everyone unites to achieve shared outcomes and celebrate successes.

Collaboration is essential for achieving shared goals, but it often comes with its own set of challenges. Addressing these challenges proactively can lead to more effective and productive teamwork. Developing the skills to mitigate these complexities are essential to leadership. Some common collaboration challenges and strategies to resolve them include:

1. Communication Breakdowns

Miscommunication, or a lack of communication, can lead to misunderstandings, missed deadlines, and frustration among team members.

Strategies to avoid these undesirable outcomes can include establishing clear methods of communicating, like emails for updates or instant messaging for quick questions. Fostering an environment of open dialogue where team members feel comfortable asking questions and providing feedback helps avoid miscommunication.

2. Conflict and Personality Clashes

Working with individuals with different values, work styles, or personalities can lead to tension and hinder collaboration.

I've learned that creating basic agreements for group interaction fosters respect and kindness. At the National Congress of Neighborhood Women, we adopted agreements through the Leadership Support Process. These include giving full attention, using I-statements, welcoming diverse perspectives, and ensuring everyone has space to share. Such agreements set clear expectations for communication and help navigate differing viewpoints thoughtfully.

When differences of opinions or conflicts arise, it is best to address them promptly before they have the chance to escalate. It's like a loose thread on a beautifully woven scarf—if you don't take care of it early, it can unravel the entire fabric. Dealing with conflicts is less stressful if you are equipped with skills to navigate and resolve disagreements. When I became a professor of Women and Gender Studies, I immediately enrolled in a training called Intentional Dialogue. I learned how to address conflict and promote effective conversations across differences. Through our social conditioning, we might learn to naturally navigate tensions with empathy, diplomacy, and a calm presence. However, training in conflict resolution can expand our toolkit with specialized skills that help us address confrontation with a balance of diplomacy and assertiveness. To enhance your leadership skills, it would be beneficial to go through some training. I know the two, half-day class I took gave me the skills to lead through conflict.

3. **Unequal Work Distribution**

When team members feel overburdened while others have less to do, frustration and inefficiency can arise. To address this, start by clearly defining roles and responsibilities so everyone understands their contributions. Regular check-ins help maintain accountability, ensure tasks are balanced, and keep the team aligned. As a leader, these check-ins are key to redistributing tasks when needed, preventing burnout, and keeping the team focused on shared goals.

I had the honor of working with a young woman, Sabrina, at an NGO (non-government organization, in this case a global, mission-driven not for profit) who organized and coordinated global meetings. She was meticulous about setting up regular check-ins around logistics, participant needs, travel arrangements, support activities, communications, etc. Her leadership ensured these meetings were both smooth and effective. However, the burden of managing all these responsibilities led to burnout, which ultimately impacted the organization.

I imagine you have had the experience of working with an individual or a group assuming everyone was completing their tasks only to find out at the deadline that someone didn't do their part. Then you are left scrambling to fill the void. It's a frustrating feeling that can usually be avoided by checking in to "see how things are going" along the way.

4. **Cultural and Language Barriers**

It's easy to assume that working toward the same goal means everyone shares the same perspective. But it's essential to recognize the different cultural norms, values, and languages that shape each person's approach. To foster collaboration, celebrate the unique strengths everyone brings to the table. Create opportunities for team members to share their lived experiences and cultural backgrounds— this builds connection, understanding, and cohesiveness. Remember, even when united by a common cause, each person brings their own values, problem-solving styles, and ways of working toward the goal.

For example, consider a woman leader managing a multicultural team working on a project to improve access to women's health care in their community. Instead of assuming everyone approaches the project with the same mindset, she actively seeks to learn about her team members' experiences and viewpoints. By asking thoughtful questions—like how cultural differences might impact how women seeking health care might react to the solutions the team proposes—she uncovers unique insights that shape more inclusive and successful outcomes.

As our world becomes more diverse and global, we need to be sensitive to language challenges of the people we work with. I work with many women whose native language is not English. I'm awed by their ability to speak English as a second language and am also careful to avoid using idiomatic expressions like "let's break the ice" to get to know someone or we don't want to "cut corners" in our work. Instead, I use simple clear words that they are more likely to have learned. It is also helpful to provide agendas and written materials before any meetings to allow participants to prepare and resolve any doubts due to language differences, as well as summaries afterwards to emphasize what was discussed and decided.

5. **Different Work and Learning Styles**

Different work and learning styles can significantly impact collaboration by influencing how team members approach tasks, process information, and communicate. For example, some individuals may prefer structured, step-by-step processes, while others thrive in flexible, dynamic environments. Similarly, visual learners might excel with charts and diagrams, while auditory learners may benefit more from discussions or verbal instructions. These differences can lead to misalignment if not acknowledged, potentially causing frustration or slowing down the collaborative process.

As a leader, it's important to understand and appreciate the different work and learning styles of the people or groups you collaborate with. By using your empathy, emotional intelligence, and relationship-building skills, you can identify and understand people's learning and work styles.

Valuing these diverse approaches can make all the difference In building strong working relationships. As I wrote earlier in the chapter, diversity enhances outcomes through better problem solving, creativity, and decision-making. Seeing these different styles as strengths and aligning tasks with capabilities creates powerful collaborations. By providing multiple ways to share ideas you can build stronger collaboration and achieve better outcomes.

6. **Remote Collaboration Challenges**

Remote collaborations often face unique challenges that can impact their effectiveness and morale. Feelings of isolation are common, as group members may lack the informal interactions and camaraderie that come naturally in a shared physical workspace. Time zone differences add another layer of complexity, making it difficult to schedule meetings or collaborate in real-time, which can lead to delays and miscommunication. Reduced engagement can also become an issue, as the physical distance and reliance on virtual tools may cause some team members to feel disconnected from the group's goals or less motivated to contribute fully.

To address the challenges faced by remote groups, implementing thoughtful strategies can significantly enhance connection, engagement, and productivity.

One key strategy is scheduling regular virtual meetings. These provide consistent opportunities for members to share updates, discuss progress, and align on goals. Regular interactions create a sense of community and mutual accountability. You can improve these meetings by ensuring they are well-structured and allow time for open discussions where all voices are heard.

Being mindful of time zones is another critical strategy for groups spread across different regions. To ensure fairness and inclusivity, you can rotate meeting times so no one consistently bears the burden of working outside regular hours. Additionally, asynchronous communication tools, like shared documents or recorded updates, can help bridge time zone gaps, allowing everyone to contribute on their schedule without feeling excluded.

Encouraging social interaction is equally important for fostering connection. In a virtual environment, informal bonding opportunities often need to be intentional. Hosting virtual social time can provide much-needed moments to connect and share. These interactions help build trust and strengthen relationships, making collaboration more enjoyable and effective.

By implementing these strategies, remote groups can overcome the barriers of distance, foster a stronger sense of belonging, and maintain high levels of engagement and collaboration.

I'm part of an incredible group called the Mission Accepted 262 Women's Project. Under the inspiring leadership of Deb Drummond, over 200 women from around the globe came together to contribute to a powerful book amplifying women's voices. But it didn't stop there—our collaboration continues through virtual summits, meetings, and active engagement on social media. Deb, Top Performance Coach, has also created a private Facebook group where we share our stories, provide support, and build connections. One of my favorite aspects is our online "ask" parties, where we can seek support from the group on anything we're working on or manifesting. We also take the time to celebrate our successes together, creating a vibrant and empowering community that uplifts each of us.

To summarize: collaboration offers immense benefits, from fostering innovation and enhancing problem solving to building stronger relationships and achieving shared goals. Bringing together diverse perspectives encourages creativity and more comprehensive solutions. However, collaboration is not without its challenges, such as communication breakdowns, workload imbalances, and cultural or work style differences. Women leaders play a crucial role in navigating these challenges by bringing empathy, emotional intelligence, and relationship-building skills to the forefront. Their ability to create inclusive environments and value diverse contributions strengthens team dynamics and drives meaningful results. By embracing clear communication, fair task distribution, and fostering mutual respect, women leaders help transform potential hurdles into opportunities for growth. Ultimately, effective collaboration, guided by strong leadership, creates an environment where everyone feels valued, aligned, and motivated to contribute to collective success.

Team Building goes beyond simply bringing together skilled individuals—it's about creating a cohesive, collaborative unit where every member feels valued, supported, and motivated to contribute their best. Effective team building requires establishing a foundation of trust, fostering open communication, and creating an environment where people feel both challenged to grow and recognized for their contributions. Women leaders are particularly effective in this area, often excelling at relationship-building and fostering mutual respect among members.

Through empathy and emotional intelligence, women leaders create spaces where individuals feel heard and understood. They often prioritize inclusivity, ensuring that diverse voices are welcomed and that everyone has a seat at the table. By recognizing the unique strengths and potential of each team member, they empower individuals to take ownership of their roles, boosting both confidence and productivity. This approach not only builds stronger bonds among members but also enhances innovation and problem solving by leveraging diverse perspectives.

I was fortunate to have a wise mentor who gave me my first opportunity in politics. Susie, a first-generation Chinese American, was the volunteer coordinator for the campaign of a local physician running for office. The volunteer coordinator is the backbone of a campaign, recruiting, training, and organizing volunteers while channeling their energy and enthusiasm into the demanding realities of political work. If you've ever worked on a campaign, you know it's intense—like a daily fire drill with constant urgency, change, and the need for flexibility.

Volunteers come with different motivations—believing in the cause, seeking access to power, or wanting to challenge the status quo. Susie had a remarkable gift for recognizing each person's strengths and uniting them into a well-oiled team, mitigating any signs of discord before conflict erupted. She could spot someone's skills or resources and inspire them to contribute for the benefit of the campaign.

At the time, I was a medical and science writer, helping doctors with journal articles and writing for magazines. Susie recruited me to draft materials on the medical issues the candidate supported. She assigned others based on their expertise—a politically connected couple handled fundraising, while others took on communications or event planning. Back then, we even had to manually prepare bulk mail, sorting it by zip code and bagging it. My five-year-old daughter loved putting stamps (or "stickers," as she called them) on the mail. When she got tired, Susie made her a cozy bed out of mailbags.

Susie kept the team motivated, celebrated small wins—like getting mail out on time or organizing successful community events—and reminded us all of our shared goal: electing Bob. Although our candidate didn't win, the tight-knit group of volunteers Susie brought together forged friendships that lasted a lifetime.

Her leadership, vision, and ability to build relationships transformed a community and created a lasting impact. Susie brought people together, provided a positive space for them to forge connections, and empowered them to take pride in their contributions. She excelled at team building by demonstrating flexibility, adaptability, and resilience, while fostering the holistic growth of team members to create a stronger, more cohesive team.

Although team building has been shown to positively impact the outcomes of groups, it can also make some people cringe because of past negative experiences. Creating an effective team building experience requires thoughtful planning, ensuring activities are inclusive, meaningful, and aligned with the group's goals while allowing space for everyone to participate comfortably.

A woman I worked with shared a story about her challenging experience during a leadership team building retreat. As the only woman on the leadership team, she wasn't included in planning the retreat. The weekend was entirely focused on physical activities like kayaking, golfing, and hiking—none of which were her preferences. Concerned about being perceived as "less than" and wanting to be part of the bonding experience, she participated in everything. However, she capsized her kayak and struggled with golf, having played only once before. Instead of fostering connection, the retreat left her feeling more isolated from the team than she had been beforehand. This is a clear example of a retreat that lacked inclusivity and consideration for diverse preferences and abilities, ultimately hindering relationship building and weakening the sense of connection within the team.

Trust Building is essential for long-term success, as it is the foundation for all relationships whether personal, professional, or with friends.

But what is trust? It is often difficult to define because everyone has different experiences with trust. According to the Cambridge dictionary, it is "the belief that someone is good and honest and will not harm you or something is safe and reliable." For me, trust is more complex than that. It is also expressed in a person's behaviors like being honest, following through with commitments or promises, and aligning their values with their actions. My relationship with trust is based on two repeated messages from my parents. My father lived by the code that "your word is your bond." My mom emphasized that "once trust is lost, it can never be fully recovered." Some might refute that sentiment, but I know in my experience, once I lost trust in someone, the relationship dynamics changed. I was never "all in" after that unless serious trust building occurred.

Trust in relationships is shaped by a mix of factors that influence both the person placing trust (the trustor), the person being trusted (the trustee), and the overall environment of their relationship. A person's capacity to trust is largely shaped by their past experiences and personal history with regards to relying on someone else. On the trustee's side, their behavior, competence, and reliability determine how trustworthy they appear. What you believe tends to manifest. Research shows that when we have confidence in someone, our actions toward them often reflect that belief. We tend to engage with them more positively than with those we doubt, offering them more opportunities to excel and providing clearer, more constructive feedback to support their progress. Additionally, we're more likely to invest time in guiding and mentoring them, trusting that our efforts will lead to meaningful results. The opposite is true when distrust exists. If we doubt the reliability of someone or our expectations are unfulfilled, we focus on their behaviors that reinforce our beliefs. People tend to withdraw, become less cooperative, and at an extreme, try to retaliate. Even efforts to rebuild trust may be viewed as suspicious. In order to maintain trust, leaders need to **model trustworthy behavior by** demonstrating honesty, fairness, and reliability.

Trust is also impacted by expectations. When expectations are met, trust increases. When they aren't one or both parties can feel betrayed. Clearly communicating and clarifying expectations is crucial to building and maintaining trust. Agreeing on what is reasonable within a relationship, whether personal or professional, requires honest and transparent conversations. It's like knowing the rules of a game. If you're on a soccer team, you need to know the rules of soccer and the expectations of the team.

Trust doesn't exist in isolation—it's shaped by shared factors like relationship dynamics, communication, and mutual understanding. Think about planning a large family holiday gathering. You coordinate responsibilities—who's bringing dishes, handling decorations, or setting the table. When everyone follows through, trust is strengthened. But if someone changes plans last minute without letting others know, or a family member consistently forgets their role, frustrations build, and distrust creeps in. Trust relies not just on individual actions but also on the context and dynamics of the group.

Trust motivates higher productivity, sparks innovation, and drives deeper engagement of those you work with, creating a thriving workplace. It serves as the cornerstone for long-term success, enabling sustainable growth and stronger relationships.

Studies show that without trust, even the most talented teams struggle to perform. People are less willing to share ideas, avoid taking risks, or struggle to collaborate effectively.

Women leading collaboration, team building, and trust building

Women lead with authenticity—actions that show their words align with their behaviors. They also create open and dependable spaces using their empathy and transparency. When I asked my daughter how she sees trust developing, she said consistency over a period of time. Our behaviors have to be trustworthy to encourage others to trust in us.

These qualities make women natural trust builders, enabling stronger connections with people in their personal and professional lives and communities. When people trust each other, they can collaborate more effectively, whether at home, work, or in other settings. Trust fosters open communication, encourages the exchange of ideas, and creates a supportive environment for problem solving. Are you someone people come to as a confidante, mentor, or for advice? Knowing it or not, you have earned a reputation for being reliable, understanding, nonjudgmental, and trustworthy.

Building trust requires attunement—the ability to tune into someone's words, body language, tone, and expressions to understand their needs. This is likely a skill you've developed through your own life experiences. As discussed in Chapter 3, women often excel in empathy and emotional intelligence, which are essential for creating strong, trusting relationships.

Women face unique challenges in building trust, often needing to work harder to prove competence in environments shaped by outdated perceptions. By demonstrating resilience, adaptability, and consistent results, we can break down stereotypes, establish credibility, and inspire trust in our leadership. Overcoming these barriers not only affirms our reliability but also reinforces the value of women in leadership roles.

Our strengths in fostering open communication, empathy, and shared goals naturally position us as trust builders. By creating inclusive spaces where people feel valued and heard, we lay the foundation for trust. Leading with emotional intelligence, authenticity, and vulnerability deepens connections and strengthens trust in both personal and professional relationships. Whether these qualities come from nature or societal influences, they enable women to effectively build and sustain trust over time.

Access to growth opportunities

Empowering women to lead requires access to development opportunities like strong mentorship and peer support networks. However, finding these resources can be a significant challenge. Women often face barriers such as limited access to leadership training based on our unique skill sets, lack of visibility in established networks, or difficulty connecting with mentors who understand our unique experiences. Overcoming these hurdles is crucial, as these resources provide the skills, guidance, and community women need to navigate challenges and step into leadership with confidence and purpose.

Fortunately, this need is becoming more recognized, and organizations are being established to strengthen the leadership journeys of women and girls. Universities, companies, and non-profits are sponsoring women's leadership academies to equip women with the skills, confidence, and networks needed to thrive in leadership roles. These programs have successfully developed strong, capable leaders who are breaking barriers, driving innovation, and fostering inclusive environments across industries and communities. Entrepreneurs like Deb Drummond are opening spaces for women's voices to be heard through her brainchild Mission Accepted 262 Women's Project.

These programs have flourished because they address a critical need to bridge the gender gap in leadership by providing women with tailored support, mentorship, and skill development.

If you haven't yet, get your free downloadable companion Workbook at cathyholt.com/unstoppableworkbook to go deeper on the chapter, write down your thoughts, and consider these takeaways and action steps.

Key Takeaways

1. The Importance of Women in Leadership

a. Women have evolved into key drivers of change, excelling at balancing results with inclusivity and compassion.

b. Overcoming challenges like stereotypes has built their resilience, adaptability, and innovation.

2. Collaboration

a. Collaboration sparks creativity and innovation by valuing diverse perspectives.

b. Women foster collaboration through empathy, active listening, and creating inclusive environments.

c. Delegating tasks aligned with strengths and celebrating shared successes enhance teamwork.

3. Team Building

a. Women excel in team building by using emotional intelligence to create cohesive, supportive groups.

b. Inclusive and thoughtfully planned activities foster connection and motivation.

4. Trust Building

a. Trust is vital for productivity, engagement, and innovation.

b. Women build trust through authenticity, consistency, and transparency, overcoming stereotypes to establish credibility.

5. Empowering Women

a. Access to professional development, mentorship, and peer support is essential but often challenging to find.

6. Why It Matters

a. Collaboration, team building, and trust building are the foundation of sustainable success, and women's strengths in these areas drive innovation, inclusivity, and meaningful results.

Action Steps to Enhance Your Skills in Collaboration, Team Building, and Trust Building

Collaboration

- **Seek Diverse Perspectives**: Engage with individuals from different backgrounds to broaden understanding and improve problem-solving.

- **Develop Active Listening Skills**: Practice listening without interrupting and acknowledging others' viewpoints to foster inclusivity.

- **Participate in Group Projects**: Join volunteer efforts, committees, or community initiatives to practice collaborative decision-making.

- **Learn to Delegate**: Assign tasks based on team members' strengths and provide clear expectations to ensure collective success.

Team Building

- **Strengthen Emotional Intelligence**: Take workshops or read about recognizing and managing emotions to improve interpersonal relationships.

- **Foster Inclusivity**: Create environments where everyone feels heard and valued by encouraging open dialogue and participation.

- **Celebrate Successes**: Acknowledge individual and team achievements to build morale and strengthen bonds.

- **Organize Team Activities**: Plan activities that align with team goals and preferences to foster connection and trust.

Trust Building

- **Be Consistent and Reliable**: Follow through on commitments and demonstrate integrity in your actions.

- **Practice Transparency**: Communicate openly about decisions, expectations, and challenges.

- **Model Vulnerability**: Share experiences and admit mistakes to build deeper connections and encourage openness.

- **Build Skills in Conflict Resolution**: Take courses or read resources on resolving disagreements to handle challenges effectively.

General Development

- **Pursue Mentorship**: Find mentors who are representative of your experiences who can guide and provide feedback on developing these skills.

- **Participate in Leadership Programs**: Attend workshops or academies focused on women's leadership to gain tools and insights.

- **Engage in Self-Reflection**: Regularly evaluate your strengths and areas for growth in collaboration, team building, and trust building.

- **Network with Peers**: Build connections with other women leaders to share experiences, strategies, and encouragement.

By taking these steps, you can enhance your ability to lead effectively and foster environments of collaboration, trust, and teamwork.

Chapter 6

Women as Problem-Solvers: Qualities That Empower Creativity and Innovation

Women as Natural Problem-Solvers

Women have always been natural problem-solvers, adept at navigating challenges in the family, workplace, and broader society. Whether coordinating the complexities of family life, managing professional demands, or driving change in their communities, women bring a unique perspective to tackling obstacles. This perspective is grounded in emotional intelligence, creativity, resilience, and holistic thinking—traits that not only enable women to solve problems but also spark innovation and progress.

Balancing multiple roles—mother, daughter, caregiver, chaos coordinator, volunteer, entrepreneur, and powerhouse professional—gives women a multidimensional view of the world. These experiences, combined with the ability to consider emotional, relational, and practical implications, allow women to uncover solutions others might miss. Women's problem solving isn't just about fixing what's broken—it's about creating pathways for growth, connection, and transformation.

The ability to address challenges holistically is one of the defining strengths of women as problem-solvers. A holistic approach to problem-solving is all about looking at the bigger picture. Instead of just fixing the obvious symptoms, it means examining how various factors—emotional, relational, practical, and systemic—interconnect and influence the problem. It's like solving a puzzle where every piece matters. By looking at problems with a broad perspective, holistic problem-solving ensures that solutions are sustainable, equitable, and aligned with broader goals, preventing unintended consequences and fostering meaningful, lasting change.

This multidimensional thinking allows women to consider not just the immediate needs, but also the long-term impact of their decisions. Whether it's a mother balancing the demands of a busy household, a leader guiding her team through a crisis, or an activist advocating for systemic change, women demonstrate an extraordinary capacity to approach problems with empathy, insight, and openness to diverse brainstorming.

Historically, women have had to navigate societal constraints and biases, which has further sharpened their problem-solving skills. They've learned to innovate within limitations, leveraging creativity and resourcefulness to overcome obstacles and achieve remarkable outcomes. In many cases, these very constraints have propelled women to think outside the box, turning challenges into opportunities

Katherine Johnson, Mary Jackson, and Dorothy Vaughan exemplify extraordinary problem-solving, perseverance, and resilience. As African-American women working at NASA during the space race in the late 1950s and early 1960s, they broke barriers of segregation, racism, and sexism while making groundbreaking contributions. Katherine Johnson's precise calculations were crucial to missions like John Glenn's orbit of Earth, Mary Jackson became NASA's first Black female engineer after petitioning to attend a whites-only program, and Dorothy

Vaughan taught herself computer programming, ensuring her team's indispensability in an evolving technological landscape.

Their brilliance extended beyond solving technical problems—they navigated systemic injustice with determination and ingenuity. Working in the shadows, they not only shaped pivotal moments in space exploration but also challenged the structures designed to exclude them. The story of their journeys in Margot Lee Shetterly's *Hidden Figures* brought long-overdue attention and accolades to these women and celebrates their resilience and brilliance while inspiring future generations to break barriers and lead with tenacity and purpose.

Problems are a fact of life. We all face challenges—big and small—that can feel overwhelming at times. Whether it's figuring out how to meet a tight deadline at work, managing a tricky personal situation, or tackling a larger issue that affects your community, problem solving is a skill we use every day. In order to reframe a problem, rather than view it as a royal pain, I try to look at them as the gap between how things are right now and how I'd like them to be. It's still work to deal with and solve them, but it gives me the perspective of impacting change.

Solving problems isn't just about jumping to answers—it's about your mindset and practices and knowing how to approach them thoughtfully and effectively.

In this chapter, we'll explore the essential skills for effective problem-solving, including critical thinking, emotional intelligence, adaptability, and collaboration—tools that empower you to tackle challenges with confidence and clarity. We'll highlight the unique qualities that make women exceptional problem-solvers and how these traits enable them to lead, innovate, and drive meaningful change.

As you read this chapter, I invite you to reflect on your strengths and identify challenges and areas for growth as we examine how to apply and cultivate these skills for even greater impact. By recognizing and celebrating your problem-solving abilities, you can unlock their full potential to create a more equitable and innovative future.

Problem-solving Steps

The first step in solving any problem is to recognize one exists and identify it clearly. This means taking the time to understand the issue and defining it in specific and concise terms. A clear definition of what exactly needs to be addressed helps avoid confusion and ensures everyone involved is focused on the same concern. It's just as important to differentiate between the symptoms of a problem and what's really causing it—referred to as the root cause.

Often, what seems to be the problem is just a surface symptom of something deeper. Using root cause analysis—asking "why" multiple times—helps uncover the underlying factors driving the issue. For example, if fewer people are attending preparation meetings for an event, you might ask:

- Why are fewer people coming?
    - The meeting times don't work for their schedules.

- Why don't the times work?
    - They conflict with work and family responsibilities.

- Why wasn't this noticed sooner?
    - We didn't ask for input on scheduling.

- Why didn't we ask for input?
    - We assumed the current schedule worked for everyone.

The real issue isn't disinterest but inconvenient timing. The solution? Gather input—perhaps through a quick poll—to find a time that works better. This approach not only resolves the issue but also strengthens engagement and collaboration within the group. By addressing root causes, you ensure solutions are both effective and sustainable.

I once attended a women's group meeting with Maimunah Mohd Sharif, the executive director of UN Habitat (the UN agency that focuses on human settlements and sustainable urban development), who shared a powerful insight: "Don't tell me what you think I need; let me tell you what I need." This simple yet profound advice reminds us to ask instead of assume, fostering deeper understanding and more effective interactions.

In my work through DEI Consultants, we often conduct community engagement sessions to get input regarding public projects. The first things we look at when scheduling the events are the demographics of the community. Are there many families with children, are both parents working, how do they traditionally get information about community events, where are places they frequent where they would be more comfortable meeting? We also survey the community to see what times would work best for them. For one project, we scheduled our community engagement in the early evening, provided supervised activities for children, and had it at a community center in the area they lived. Asking questions rather than assuming helped us solve our problem of attendance.

The next step in solving a problem is to gather information. In the example of our community engagements I just mentioned, the demographic facts we gathered informed our decisions for the problem of how to get people to our community engagements. Talking to the people directly affected by the problem is key. It provides you with their perspectives, uncovers details you might have missed, and builds a more complete picture of the situation.

It's also important to take a step back and look at the bigger picture. Think about how far-reaching the problem is and what the potential consequences might be. This way, you're not just tackling the surface issue but also uncovering any deeper factors or possible ripple effects. When you have a clear understanding of the full context, you'll be in a much stronger position to make thoughtful decisions and find solutions that really work.

For example, imagine you're a woman entrepreneur noticing declining sales in your business. While the surface issue seems to be low customer interest, a deeper analysis uncovers ripple effects: inconsistent marketing has hurt brand visibility, lowered team morale, and decreased productivity, with some employees even considering leaving. Addressing just the symptom—like offering discounts or running more disjointed marketing campaigns—won't resolve the root causes.

A friend of mine, Lisa Raebel, highlights this in her book *The Rebel Girl's Guide to Marketing*, where she warns against "Random Acts of Marketing." She emphasizes the importance of knowing where you want your marketing to take you before creating a plan. As the leader of your business, this means evaluating your current marketing efforts: Are they effective? What is your marketing goal? It also involves examining team dynamics and morale to identify what's affecting productivity. By gathering this critical information and addressing the underlying issues, you can develop solutions that resolve the root problem rather than just masking the symptoms.

After you've gathered as much information currently available about the problem, the next step in problem-solving is getting clear on what you're working toward—your goals. Defining your goals means asking yourself: What does success look like in this situation? Whether it's solving a specific problem, hitting a target, changing something you don't like, or solving a relationship issue, having a clear outcome in mind gives you direction and purpose. Once you know your goal, it's just as important to establish how you'll measure success. Think about how you'll know your solution is working—maybe it's hitting a specific number, noticing a change in behavior, or hearing positive feedback from others. Having clear goals and measures of success gives you a solid roadmap to guide your decisions and keep track of your progress as you go.

After you have defined your problem and the root causes, gathered intel, and figured out your goals, you are ready to brainstorm solutions. The key to brainstorming is to let creativity flow without holding back or overthinking. This is the moment to think outside the box and consider every possibility, even the ideas that might seem a little unconventional at first. Visionary and creative thinking are powerful tools for solving problems because they allow people to imagine new possibilities and break free from conventional approaches. Visionary thinking helps you see the bigger picture, set long-term goals, and anticipate future challenges, while creative thinking brings fresh, out-of-the-box ideas to the table.

Women are particularly strong in these areas thanks to our holistic approach, which takes emotional, relational, and practical factors into account (as I addressed earlier in the chapter). Our empathy allows us to anticipate others' needs, and their experience navigating barriers has sharpened their ability to innovate within constraints.

As women, we create spaces that are more inclusive and use our creativity to find practical, impactful ways to bring ideas to life. This combination of vision and creativity allows women to tackle problems with ingenuity and make meaningful change.

Involving other people can make a huge difference—getting diverse perspectives can spark ideas you might not have thought of on your own. I love brainstorming in groups. Sometimes other people can see our problems more clearly than we can, and their perspectives open up new possibilities.

Collaboration often leads to the most innovative solutions. Make sure to write everything down, no matter how wild or small the idea seems; sometimes the best answers come from a spark that didn't feel obvious at first. This is all about exploring options and seeing where your creativity takes you.

Once you've brainstormed these possible solutions, you need to evaluate them. This means taking a close look at each option and weighing the pros and cons—think about how realistic it is, what it will cost, and the potential impact it could have. It's also important to consider any risks or challenges that might come with each choice, so you can be prepared to address them. Finally, make sure the solution aligns with your goals and the criteria you've set for success. After considering all the ramifications and sometimes unintended consequences, it is time to choose the best solution. You know your goal and have defined what success will look like. By carefully assessing your options, you'll feel confident about picking a path forward that truly addresses the problem.

Now that you know your solution, it's time to develop an action plan. Creating an action plan is about figuring out the steps you need to take to make your solution happen—like a roadmap. Start by breaking the solution into manageable tasks, so you know exactly what needs to be done and in what order. If you're working with a group, delegate (Chapter 5). Assign responsibilities to ensure everyone involved knows their role and set realistic deadlines to keep things moving forward and to stay on track. A good action plan keeps everything organized and helps you focus on getting the problem solved step by step.

Once you have a plan, you need to implement—that's where ideas meet action. I don't know about you, but that's where I sometimes stumble. Just getting it done isn't always easy. It's work, sometimes uncomfortable... but I know that if I don't deal with the problem, it festers and usually increases in scope and severity. Procrastinating can also lead to stress and anxiety, or result in me missing opportunities that present themselves after the problem is solved. That's where timelines are helpful at keeping us on track. In my work with Julie Miller Davis, Founder, CEO, JMD Productivity Training, I have learned the art of "reverse chunking." The idea is to start with the deadline you want to meet and work backward from there. By breaking the project into smaller tasks and assigning specific times to complete each one, you create a clear, manageable plan to reach your goal on time. Although timelines aren't always set in stone, it is important to stay on track by monitoring progress and paying attention to the milestones you set, understanding that adjustments might be needed. Effective communication is key during this phase. Keeping everyone updated on progress, whether it's celebrating successes, addressing setbacks, or outlining next steps, promotes transparency and keeps the process moving forward. Implementation is more than just completing tasks; it's about staying involved and adaptable to make sure the solution achieves the problem-solving goal.

Imagine you're that chaos coordinator and notice that your family is constantly stressed by overlapping schedules, missed activities, and frustration. You identify the problem as a lack of a centralized way to track commitments and gather input from everyone about their weekly routines. Your goal is to create a system to reduce conflicts, and after brainstorming solutions like a whiteboard, weekly meetings, or a shared calendar app, you choose the app so that everyone can use it. You set it up, add commitments, and introduce it during a family meeting while explaining how to use it. Over time, with consistent use and minor adjustments, the shared calendar reduces scheduling conflicts, improves communication, and brings more harmony to the household.

Problem solving is a lot like planning a trip—it's all about figuring out where you want to go and how to get there. First, you identify your destination, much like defining the problem and what you're trying to achieve. Then, you gather information: research your options, map out routes, and learn about your destination, similar to understanding the context and collecting data about the problem.

Next, you brainstorm different ways to get there—will you drive, fly, or take a train? This mirrors generating potential solutions. Once you've listed your options, you weigh the pros and cons—considering cost, time, and convenience—just as you evaluate solutions to determine the best fit. Finally, you make your choice, create an itinerary, and off you go, much like implementing your plan to solve the problem. When you're back home, you likely think about whether the trip fulfilled your travel bug—if you would have done something differently like a different destination or whether next time you might fly rather than drive.

Just like a trip, solving a problem requires flexibility. If a road is closed or a flight is delayed, you adjust your plan. Similarly, with problem solving, you may need to refine your approach as new challenges arise. Both processes are about preparation, decision-making, and finding the best path forward to reach your goal.

In my experience, the last step of evaluating the outcome is often left out of the process because we've solved the problem and we're celebrating our success. But to improve your problem-solving skills, it is important to evaluate the process and results of your efforts.

Did the results meet the criteria for success you initially identified? Look at what worked and what didn't, and analyze why. What did you learn from your efforts? Are there things you could have done differently to improve the process or results? Use these lessons learned to refine your approach for future challenges. This step is not just about measuring success, but about learning and improving for next time.

Finally, you need to celebrate your successes. Sometimes I have to remind myself of this. I'm thrilled I solved a problem, but immediately start focusing on the next issue that needs addressing. To help me break this habit and celebrate my success, my friend Julie encourages me to text her my victories, no matter how small I think they are.

This structured approach may seem cumbersome, but in reality, we often do it organically for smaller scale problems in our personal lives. If you've ever had a dinner party, you've probably gone through these steps. You want to make a dish that satisfies everyone's tastes and dietary restrictions (identified the problem). You ask your guests about allergies, check to see what ingredients you have and need, and figure out how much time you're going to need to cook the food (information gathering). You may not have thought of it this way, but you've defined the goal as creating a meal that's delicious, accommodates dietary needs, and fits within your budget and available time. You brainstorm possible dishes (solutions) and compare the ideas you've come up with based on the information you gathered (ingredients, time, guests' dietary needs). You write a shopping list, prep ingredients, and schedule cooking time before guests arrive (action plan). You're implementing your solution when you cook the meal, adjusting as needed and serving it to your guests. When you get feedback from the guests, you're evaluating the outcome.

Even small decisions like this benefit from a structured problem-solving process, helping you make thoughtful choices and adapt to any challenges. And a structure is particularly important when working with others to make sure the process is thorough, collaborative, and effective, leading to sustainable and impactful solutions.

Core Qualities of Women as Problem-Solvers

Most experts that coach or consult on problem solving agree that there is usually an emotional component to problems.

Whether you are trying to solve a problem individually or in a group, your experiences in life shape your feelings about the problem.

I was facilitating a UN expert group meeting with about 40 global advocates for women's issues, specifically addressing violence against women. The goal was to brainstorm how women's groups could challenge systemic barriers to reducing violence and collaborate with power structures to create change. The discussion revealed how deeply personal experiences shaped perspectives on the issue. Women who had survived domestic abuse viewed the problem differently than those who had been raped outside the home, while survivors of sexual violence during armed conflicts brought a unique emotional depth to the conversation. Those who had never personally experienced violence, including men and women wanting to act as allies, approached the issue with a different emotional lens, which also influenced their ideas. Each perspective added a valuable layer of complexity to understanding the root causes and brainstorming solutions.

As discussed in Chapter 3, emotional intelligence equips individuals with self-awareness, self-regulation, empathy, social skills, and intrinsic motivation to navigate emotions and relationships effectively. And women tend to score high on this quality. Empathy is one of the most prominent aspects of emotional intelligence. It allows us to tune into the emotions and perspectives of others, helping them uncover the root causes of conflicts or problems. It also motivates us with a genuine desire to solve problems and create meaningful and inclusive change.

Facilitating this discussion on violence against women was monumentally difficult for me. I was aware that I did not have the experience of being assaulted. But their stories deeply impacted me, and I had to control my horror at hearing their stories. The social skills of the group had created a sense of trust to be vulnerable and a desire to collaborate. My empathy for these women who were sharing their stories increased my motivation to find solutions to this monumental problem.

I also had to acknowledge that my emotions were affecting my ability to lead this process. My natural empathy made me highly attuned to the needs and emotions of others, which is a valuable strength. However, it can sometimes make it harder to make tough decisions, especially if those decisions might upset others or create temporary discomfort. Balancing empathy with the ability to make objective, outcome-focused decisions can be a challenge. In the end, I enlisted the support of another facilitator in order to advance the process towards our goal of finding ways to reduce the violence women were experiencing at home and around the world. The two of us were able to shepherd the group to focus their experiences and perspectives to achieve the goal of identifying recommendations to address violence against women.

Emotional intelligence enables women to navigate emotions and relationships with finesse, making them effective at understanding and addressing challenges. Empathy plays a key role, allowing women to uncover root causes of issues and find meaningful solutions. At the same time, we have to be aware of the need to balance EQ and empathy with objectivity when we are solving problems. Being too emotional can be just as detrimental to finding sustainable solutions as being too clinical and logical.

Women also score high on the ability to thinking holistically about problems. By examining situations through emotional, relational, and practical lenses, women often uncover solutions that might otherwise be missed. This multidimensional approach enables them to address immediate needs while also considering the broader, long-term effects of their decisions. But looking at the bigger picture and considering various perspective can sometimes lead to overanalyzing or feeling overwhelmed by the sheer complexity of a problem. Focusing on every detail and potential outcome might delay decision-making or create self-doubt.

A group of women I worked with identified a lack of education for girls in their slum-dwelling community about menstruation, leading to widespread myths, shame, and misinformation. Jane, who lived in the slum, organized a team to provide fact-based education, addressing not only knowledge gaps, but also issues like hygiene, access to products, privacy, and social perceptions of sexual readiness. Girls were being told that they shouldn't be physically active during their period, couldn't bath or swim during that time of the month, or they were just being moody and irrational if they experienced PMS. Initially overwhelmed by the breadth of challenges, the group prioritized what could be tackled immediately with available resources while planning for broader collaborations.

Their program, PolycomGirls, now supports 6,000 girls annually and distributes over 10,000 sanitary supplies. It has expanded to include initiatives for women's empowerment, economic development, and ending violence against women, as well as engaging boys and men as gender champions. This evolution demonstrates women's ability to creatively problem-solve, adapt, and leverage limited resources to drive meaningful change, showcasing their resilience and innovation as agents of transformation. And Jane is now a Global Peace Ambassador, community mobilizer, speaker, and influencer in African and global platforms.

As women we also score high on communication skills and fostering collaboration. Our ability to effectively listen and articulate needs allows us to rally others around solutions.

I have had the good fortune of working with several women who are master communicators. Their ability to communicate challenges and rally people around solutions have had a major impact on the world.

My friend Jan was a product of the early women's movement, working with women like Gloria Steinem and Bella Abzug. Her passion for women's equality not just in the US, but globally, fueled her vision to form a global women's movement. She co-founded her first women's organizations, National Congress of Neighborhood Women, in the early 1970s. Their main objective was to empower poor and working-class women to step into leadership roles within their communities—amplifying their voices, raising awareness of their own strength, and equipping them to identify and address the challenges their communities faced. After participating in several global meetings, Jan noticed a dearth of poor and working-class women attending and sharing their perspectives. Although programs and projects were being discussed to address issues of poverty and women, their voices weren't represented or heard. In 1995, at a UN meeting, she and several of her collaborators lobbied the Secretary General to create an organization for grassroots women. The Huairou Commission was born.

Throughout these life events, Jan used her ability to communicate the challenges of poor and working-class women and how their perspectives were integral to creating programs that empowered them with agency and opportunities to improve their lives and the lives of their families and communities. Not only did she rally women to join this movement, but she also created allies in the global power structures to collaborate with these women. Every time I listen to her talk about women's rights and empowerment, I am motivated to join and do more. She has built relationships worldwide that problem-solve around women's empowerment, always ensuring that women are at the decision-making table. Both the National Congress of Neighborhood Women and the Huairou Commission gained consulting status with the United Nations.

Consensus-building is a powerful tool for fostering collaboration and inclusivity, but if not managed well, it can hinder effective problem-solving. The process of achieving unanimous agreement can delay decisions, especially in urgent situations. In trying to satisfy everyone, solutions may become watered down, addressing only parts of the problem without fully resolving it. Groupthink can also emerge, where the desire for harmony suppresses diverse perspectives and limits creativity. Dominant personalities might overshadow quieter contributors, reducing the range of ideas considered. Additionally, the emphasis on agreement can lead to avoiding conflict, leaving deeper issues unresolved and bold or unconventional solutions unexplored. For consensus-building to be effective, it's crucial to balance inclusivity with decisiveness, ensuring that the process fosters diverse input while driving meaningful and high-quality outcomes.

Other challenges to problem solving can include breaking down societal biases that limit our potential as problem-solvers and getting out of our own way.

Emotional intelligence and empathy are often undervalued in traditional decision-making environments, where assertiveness or logic is prioritized. Sometimes we may face challenges in having emotionally informed insights taken seriously, especially in male-dominated spaces. To address these perceptions of emotional intelligence as a weakness, we can reinforce how empathy and emotionally informed insights are strategic tools that improve decision-making, foster collaboration, resolve conflicts, and lead to more comprehensive and effective outcomes.

Sometimes we also sabotage ourselves by feeling like we need to present flawless solutions due to societal or internalized pressures. This sense of perfectionism can lead to hesitation or reluctance to make decisions without feeling fully prepared. This can create barriers to quick and effective problem-solving. To overcome the pressure of perfectionism, focus on progress over perfection by embracing a growth mindset, acknowledging that mistakes are part of the learning process, and prioritizing timely decision-making over flawless execution.

Moving forward, it is important to acknowledge that cultivating and enhancing problem-solving skills involves developing a combination of self-awareness, continuous learning, collaboration, and adaptability.

Self-awareness and mindfulness are foundational, as understanding one's strengths and growth areas allows individuals to approach problems with confidence and clarity. Mindfulness practices, such as journaling or meditation, can improve focus and emotional regulation, helping to stay calm under pressure.

Lifelong learning is equally important; staying curious and open to acquiring new knowledge or skills broadens the scope of potential solutions. For example, many women have leveraged additional education or professional development opportunities to tackle challenges with fresh perspectives.

Building support networks of mentors, peers, and allies adds another layer of strength, as these networks offer diverse viewpoints and encourage innovative thinking through collaboration.

At the same time, strategic risk-taking helps develop the confidence to embrace challenges and step outside comfort zones. Techniques like weighing potential outcomes or starting with smaller calculated risks can make stepping into the unknown more manageable.

Finally, balancing analytical and creative thinking ensures a well-rounded approach to problem-solving. Logic provides structure, while creativity introduces fresh ideas. Engaging in activities like brainstorming workshops or design thinking exercises helps integrate these two approaches, leading to comprehensive and effective solutions. Together, these qualities form a powerful toolkit for addressing challenges in a thoughtful, dynamic, and impactful way.

If you haven't yet, get your free downloadable companion Workbook at cathyholt.com/unstoppableworkbook to go deeper on the chapter, write down your thoughts, and consider these takeaways and action steps.

Key Takeaways

1. Unique Strengths:
Women excel in problem-solving with emotional intelligence, creativity, resilience, and holistic thinking, allowing them to address challenges comprehensively and innovate effectively.

2. Holistic Approach:
A broad perspective enables women to address root causes, consider long-term impacts, and create sustainable, inclusive solutions.

3. Asking the Right Questions:
Techniques like root cause analysis uncover deeper issues, fostering clarity and collaboration. Listening to those directly affected ensures more effective solutions.

4. Steps to Problem-Solving:
- Clearly define the problem.
- Gather information and perspectives.
- Analyze root causes.
- Set goals and success criteria.
- Brainstorm and evaluate solutions.
- Implement and monitor progress.

5. Collaboration and Communication:
Strong communication skills and collaboration enable women to rally teams, amplify diverse voices, and foster innovative outcomes.

6. Balancing Empathy and Objectivity:
Emotional intelligence is a strength, but balancing empathy with objectivity ensures effective and outcome-driven decisions.

7. Adaptability and Resilience:
Women's ability to adapt and stay resilient in dynamic circumstances drives their success in solving complex problems.

8. Learning and Growth:
Continuous learning, self-awareness, and strategic risk-taking enhance problem-solving capabilities, fostering confidence and innovation.

9. Celebrate and Reflect:
Recognizing successes and reflecting on lessons learned reinforces growth and inspires future leadership.

Action Steps for Women to Develop Problem-Solving Skills

1. Leverage Unique Strengths:

a. Reflect on how emotional intelligence, creativity, and resilience have helped you solve challenges in the past.

b. Actively practice using these traits in new situations.

2. Adopt a Holistic Perspective:

a. Practice looking at challenges from multiple angles: emotional, relational, practical, and systemic.

b. Ask yourself how your decisions might impact others in the short and long term to ensure sustainable and inclusive solutions.

3. Master the Art of Asking Questions:

a. Apply root cause analysis by repeatedly asking "why" to uncover the deeper causes of issues.

b. Cultivate a habit of asking thoughtful, open-ended questions when collaborating with others to gain diverse perspectives.

4. Follow Problem-Solving Steps:

a. Practice defining problems clearly before diving into solutions.

b. Break challenges into manageable tasks and monitor progress regularly.

5. Enhance Collaboration and Communication:

a. Actively listen to others' perspectives and encourage quieter voices to contribute.

b. Develop your ability to articulate problems and rally others toward solutions that align with shared goals.

6. Balance Empathy with Objectivity:

a. Recognize when empathy is driving your decisions and evaluate if it aligns with the desired outcomes.

7. Build Adaptability and Resilience:

a. View challenges as opportunities to grow and embrace change with a flexible mindset.

b. Reflect on past setbacks to identify lessons learned and ways to improve in future situations.

8. Commit to Lifelong Learning and Growth:

a. Attend workshops, enroll in courses, seek feedback, or read about problem-solving techniques to expand your skill set.

9. Celebrate and Reflect on Successes:

a. Take time to recognize your achievements, both big and small, to boost confidence and motivation.

b. After solving a problem, reflect on what worked well and what could be improved to enhance your future problem-solving capabilities.

By taking these intentional steps, we can build on our strengths, develop new skills, and become even more effective at addressing challenges and leading transformative change in our lives and communities.

Chapter 7

Adaptability Is an Essential Leadership Quality

Leadership today is more complex and demanding than ever, especially for women navigating diverse roles in their personal and professional lives. In a world shaped by rapid technological advancements, global interconnectedness, and constant challenges, thriving as a leader requires more than just a plan— it calls for adaptability and resilience. Whether managing a household, championing community initiatives, or stepping into leadership roles in business or nonprofit spaces, women face a unique mix of opportunities and barriers. From breaking through systemic challenges to fostering meaningful change, women are called to lead with creativity, courage, and a dynamic skill set that meets the complexities of modern life.

Adaptability is the ability to remain flexible, embrace change, and make adjustments when things don't go as planned. It's thinking on your feet, being resourceful, and being ready to pivot and adjust course when life takes an unexpected turn. Adaptive leaders learn to step out of their comfort zones, embrace feedback, and continuously learn. They inspire the people they work with by demonstrating that change isn't something to fear, but an opportunity for growth. It's the skill that keeps you moving forward and navigating change.

It often means adapting new strategies in response to new challenges or opportunities. It's being open to change, learning from experience, and staying curious about what's next. For example, women who transitioned to working remotely during COVID-19 often took on more household, family, and child care responsibilities. Online group calls with intermittent interruptions of curious children and pets became the norm.

Resilience, on the other hand, is about perseverance and recovery. It's your inner fire. It's what keeps you going when the going gets tough. It's about picking yourself up after a setback, learning from it, and coming back even stronger. Resilient leaders create stability and inspire confidence in their personal and professional relationships, showing that adversity can be a catalyst for strength and innovation.

For women leaders, resilience often emerges through lived experiences. We navigate gender biases, overcome systemic barriers, break through glass ceilings, or balance professional and personal responsibilities while staying focused on long-term goals. Whether it's managing rejection, tackling imposter syndrome, or dealing with the pressures of balancing multiple roles, resilience empowers leaders to not only survive adversity but thrive beyond it.

What makes these two qualities so powerful is the way they work together. Adaptability enables leaders to stay flexible and open to change, while resilience gives them the inner strength and determination to push through challenges. Together, they create a cycle of growth and progress, helping leaders tackle uncertainty. For women, this dynamic is especially powerful. The ability to juggle multiple responsibilities, handle expectations, and apply empathy and understanding when dealing with challenges often builds adaptability and resilience. These aren't just survival skills—they're your superpowers. Whether you're blazing a trail as an entrepreneur or finding your voice as an emerging leader, mastering these traits can open doors, inspire others, and take you to heights you never imagined.

This chapter focuses on adaptability, a critical quality for effective leadership, particularly in today's ever-changing world. While resilience plays a complementary role, this chapter will specifically explore the dynamics of adaptability and its unique impact on leadership. Women often bring natural strengths like emotional intelligence, multitasking, and collaborative problem-solving, which enhance their ability to adapt to shifting circumstances. By cultivating adaptability, women can lead with confidence, creativity, and purpose, positioning themselves to navigate uncertainty and inspire meaningful change. Resilience, a closely connected trait, will be explored in greater depth in the next chapter.

Part 1: Understanding Adaptability in Leadership

Defining Adaptability

As I have already written, adaptability is a skill we all use, whether we realize it or not. It's how we adjust to change, think creatively, and find ways to move forward when life doesn't go as planned. Adaptability means being able to shift your mindset, actions, and emotions to handle uncertainty or change effectively. It involves adjusting your thinking to see challenges as opportunities for growth, modifying your behavior to navigate new circumstances, and managing your feelings to stay grounded and positive. By being flexible in these areas, you can approach change with confidence and find solutions even in unfamiliar or unpredictable situations. It's about maintaining a sense of calm and staying open, resourceful, and focused on your goals when the unexpected happens.

But it's more than just adjusting when things change. It's about learning new skills and preparing yourself to handle whatever challenges or opportunities come your way.

Finding the courage to face the things you fear is closely tied to adaptability, as both require a willingness to step outside your comfort zone and embrace uncertainty. Courage propels you to confront challenges, while adaptability helps you adjust to the new realities that emerge when you do. Together, they create a powerful combination that enables growth and resilience in the face of change.

In leadership, adaptability is essential for navigating uncertainty, but it's something we practice in our personal lives too.

Think about learning to parent. No matter how many books you read or how much advice you get, real life with children is full of surprises. You might have planned a peaceful day at the park, but a sudden tantrum or an unexpected rainstorm forces you to pivot. Parents learn quickly how to think on their feet, problem solve, and adjust their expectations—all while keeping their kids safe and happy. That's adaptability in action.

And, according to an article in Forbes magazine—a global media company that focuses on business, investing, technology, and entrepreneurship—adaptability is the "single most important trait great leaders possess."

Almost 3,000 years ago a Greek philosopher, Heraclitus, coined the phrase (obviously since translated to English) "Change is the only constant in life." This pre-Aristotle and Plato thought leader must have gotten it right if we still use his quote.

The sooner we realize that nothing stays the same forever, the easier it'll be to welcome and embrace changes when they occur. Endings and beginnings are happening in every single moment. And how you react to change will affect your state of being, your relationships, and your ability to work and lead.

Change can trigger a wide range of feelings. A natural reaction is often resistance. Other feelings can include sadness, anxiety, stress, or fear. Fear can often freeze us in our tracks. Not being able to see the future that lies ahead makes us pause. We know the past, even with all its ups and downs. But what lies ahead? Will this new path lead us to unpleasantness, hurt, danger...? And when change is out of our control, it can trigger feelings of anger and frustration. Resisting change can close the door to new opportunities or blind us to possibilities that might lead to growth and success.

Other people may face change with excitement and an expectation of new adventures. That doesn't mean that they don't experience apprehension, but they view change with a growth mindset—that they are capable of learning and adapting, and that good things will happen. New adventures might mean new ideas, creative problem-solving, better relationships, personal growth—the list is extensive.

Having a growth mindset allows us to adapt and thrive. It also gives us confidence in addressing change. It helps us cultivate an attitude of trust in ourselves—that all we have survived and overcome in our lives up to now has prepared us to handle whatever is next. And it allows us to trust more in our decision-making ability. Even if we've been bruised and scratched up in the past, we will likely grow and find light in the new experience. We are adaptable and resilient.

Being flexible and forward-thinking not only helps you tackle challenges, but is also a quality that is essential both personally and professionally.

How many people do you recall feeling comfortable with online work meetings or virtual family chats in 2020, before the pandemic changed everything? Yet today, digital face-to-face communication has become second nature for people of all generations. In just a few short years, hundreds of millions adapted to the unexpected challenge of working, socializing, and staying connected without in-person interaction—a powerful example of how quickly we can embrace change when circumstances demand it.

Adapting to change with a positive mindset when it's time to pivot is a true display of leadership strength.

What if you're a small business owner who has been gearing up for months to open a brick-and-mortar store, investing time and money into the perfect location. Just as you're ready to launch, everything is shut down because of the pandemic. How many in-person businesses and restaurants faced this reality with COVID-19?

In this moment, you have to quickly adapt—rethinking your strategy to include online sales, delivery options, or pop-up events in different outdoor locations. It's a stressful, high-stakes situation, but how you approach the challenge will affect your whole team. Imagine if you freak out, have a meltdown, and start fearing your life's work will fail.

I imagine your inner voice might be sharing all of those emotions, but it is important to not convey them to your team. Staying calm, communicating with your team your determination to make it work, brainstorming with them about other possibilities, and pivoting creatively can turn what feels like a disaster into a new opportunity to expand your reach.

Success in these situations, whether for you individually or as a leader, comes from being open to change, finding creative ways to settle in, and staying optimistic despite the challenges. These moments require flexibility, resilience, and a willingness to embrace the unknown.

Components of Adaptability

Adaptability might seem like a single skill, but it's really made up of several important traits that help you adjust and thrive, whether at work or in everyday life.

Flexibility

Flexibility and adaptability are closely related but distinct concepts that work hand in hand. Flexibility focuses on the ability to adjust quickly in the moment. It's about shifting plans, accommodating new ideas, or finding alternative solutions when immediate circumstances require a change. Flexibility is an essential skill for handling day-to-day disruptions or sudden shifts in direction. It's not about abandoning your goals, just finding new ways to achieve them.

Adaptability, however, is a broader and more dynamic quality. It includes the quick adjustments of flexibility along with other traits I will discuss in coming pages.

While flexibility helps you adjust to immediate changes, adaptability equips you to thrive in environments of ongoing uncertainty and complexity. It's the ability to learn from challenges, anticipate future needs, and continuously evolve your approach to meet shifting demands.

For example, imagine you're both an entrepreneur and a mother. You're working on a critical project for your business, with a tight deadline looming, when you get a call that your child is sick and needs to be picked up from school.

Flexibility in this scenario means quickly reworking your schedule for the day—perhaps pushing a client meeting to the afternoon or rescheduling less urgent tasks—so you can take care of your child while still addressing the most pressing aspects of your project.

Adaptability involves stepping back to reassess how recurring challenges impact your long-term goals. Recognizing a pattern, you might create a sustainable strategy, such as hiring part-time help, building a reliable team to delegate tasks, or seeking support from your personal network during emergencies. This proactive approach helps your business thrive while enabling you to manage the unpredictability of family responsibilities effectively.

When my daughter was in elementary and junior high school, I was often working out of town, and her dad, a busy surgeon, couldn't exactly pause mid-surgery for a school emergency. So I got creative and teamed up with a group of other moms to form an "emergency response squad." We'd step in, handle the emergency, and take care of each other's children until the respective parent could get there. It was like having a safety net of supermoms! It was such a relief knowing we had each other to depend on for those everyday surprises life loves to throw at parents.

Flexibility helped us handle the immediate challenge of balancing competing priorities, but adaptability allowed us to take a broader view, create systems that support our long-term success, and thrive through these experiences. Together, these qualities empowered us to manage our many roles and be responsive.

Communication

Effective communication is one of the foundations of adaptability. Clear communication helps people adapt to unexpected changes by providing the information and understanding they need to process the situation, align their efforts, and respond effectively, especially when the change is not within their circle of control. Such reassurance can spark their commitment to a positive outcome. By addressing how adjustments will impact individuals and emphasizing the importance of their roles, communication strategies can rally support and drive successful implementation.

As discussed in Chapter 4, communication shapes how leaders inspire, influence, and connect with others. Clear and effective communication builds trust, aligns efforts, and motivates individuals or teams to work toward shared goals. During disruptions of the status quo, it is doubly important that leaders express their ideas clearly, both verbally and in writing, ensuring that their message resonates and fosters collaboration.

People involved in change usually want to know why there is a need for change and how the change will affect them. Understanding the reason behind a change can help reduce resistance and encourage people to actively engage in finding solutions. Open and honest communication fosters trust and encourages commitment to implementing new strategies or adjustments. It can also reduce rumors and distrust.

Chapter 4 delves more deeply into adapting communication style to suit different audiences, whether it's engaging with people from diverse backgrounds, roles, or locations. Part of this adaptation should include balancing the rationale for change with the emotional components of the audience. Actively listening (yes—that again) to feedback and concerns should play a role in adapting your message.

Imagine a family learning that a loved one has decided to move to another state for a new job. Adapting to this new reality might involve having open conversations about how to stay connected despite the distance. Family members could discuss schedules for regular video calls, plan visits, or find ways to celebrate milestones remotely. By openly sharing feelings and brainstorming solutions together, the family uses communication to adapt to the new situation while maintaining strong bonds.

Clear and open communication is at the heart of adaptability. Being able to effectively communicate the "why" behind a shift, address concerns, and rally people around a new direction is a key leadership skill. But communication isn't just about giving instructions; it's about listening as well. Taking the time to understand others' perspectives fosters trust and collaboration, which are critical during times of change. Transparent and empathetic communication makes transitions smoother and helps everyone involved stay cohesive and motivated.

Continuous Learning

Adaptability thrives when we commit to continuous learning, and this mindset is something anyone can embrace in their personal or professional life. By staying open to new knowledge, skills, and perspectives, we equip ourselves to handle change with greater confidence and ease. It also demonstrates a willingness to grow and an openness to new experiences, and sparks curiosity for what could be rather than what is.

Choosing to embrace continuous learning is not only practical but also empowering. It reinforces the idea that we are not confined by past experiences or limited by current circumstances. Instead, it highlights our ability to grow and adapt to the challenges and opportunities that life presents. It keeps us relevant in this rapidly changing world. Whether through formal education, seeking guidance, or learning from daily experiences, a commitment to learning fosters a sense of capability and readiness for what lies ahead. Lifelong learning can show up as learning how to use a new app, picking up a hobby, or trying a different approach to a problem. Each small step toward growth helps us become more flexible and resilient. It's not about achieving perfection, but about embracing progress and staying open to new possibilities.

Continuous learning provides other benefits to our personal growth. Learning new knowledge and gaining exposure to new perspectives and experiences better equips us in problem-solving and creative thinking. It sharpens our critical thinking and informs our decision-making. In our professional lives, it positions us to be more competitive and exposes you to career opportunities you might not have initially considered.

Mino, from Madagascar, shared her experiences as a woman in a culture where she was expected to be seen, but not heard. After acquiring her degrees in economic development and finance and training in human resource management, she began consulting for organizations like the World Bank and World Food Program, evaluating, monitoring, and reporting on projects. When she took a job as the executive director of an African non-profit, she was challenged about her leadership because of biases of being young, a woman, and unmarried without a family.

"We are not supposed to be defined by our role in society, but by our skills and experiences," she said. Such discrimination led her to learn more about women's rights, especially as she saw other women being denied opportunities. She then became an activist for women's rights and facilitated leadership trainings for other women to find their voices. She credits lifelong learning as a tool for her career development. She is now an African regional coordinator for several NGOs and global leader on gender equity, microfinancing for women, land rights, and climate change. Through continuous learning, she doesn't harbor set ideas but constantly wants to learn other perspectives and challenge norms.

Leaders who prioritize learning are better equipped to respond to change because they actively seek out new knowledge, skills, and perspectives. Promoting lifelong learning sparks those you work with to expand their knowledge and horizons. It also demonstrates a willingness to grow and improve, which sets an example for others.

Continuous learning fosters agility, allowing you to stay ahead of trends and adapt to shifting circumstances with confidence. A mindset of constantly learning ensures that you remain adaptable in any environment.

Cultivating a Forward-Thinking Mindset

A forward-thinking mindset is about looking beyond immediate challenges to anticipate future possibilities and opportunities. It involves staying curious, open to new ideas, and willing to explore innovative solutions. This mindset encourages a focus on growth, learning, and long-term outcomes, helping people and groups navigate uncertainty using knowledge and experiences. By combining curiosity, a growth-oriented perspective, and strategic foresight, a forward-thinking mindset empowers people to adapt to change while staying focused on what lies ahead. It is a cornerstone of adaptability.

Curiosity is the spark that drives innovation and adaptability. When we approach challenges with curiosity, we see them as opportunities to explore, experiment, and discover new solutions. Curiosity encourages us to ask questions, seek feedback, and look beyond the obvious for creative answers. It pushes us to stay engaged and open-minded, even when things don't go as planned. By cultivating curiosity, we create space where exploration and innovation are not just encouraged but celebrated, paving the way for adaptability to flourish.

A growth mindset is the belief that abilities and intelligence can be developed through effort and learning. We can change! When we embrace a growth mindset, we view challenges and see setbacks as opportunities to learn and improve. We become more willing to try new approaches to addressing challenges. We learn to welcome feedback as a way to continuously improve. When we believe in our ability to grow, we can adapt to new situations and navigate change from a place of confidence in our knowledge and with determination.

Strategic foresight is the ability to look ahead and identify potential challenges and opportunities, which is a cornerstone of adaptability. This is what I call brainstorming what-ifs and having a plan B. It means spotting trends, considering other possible outcomes and unintended consequences that might surface, and planning for different scenarios so you're ready for whatever comes your way. It combines critical thinking with creative problem-solving to stay ahead of potential change and position yourself for long-term success. It raises your awareness of what could happen and prepares you to be proactive rather than scrambling to react to surprises. You are ready for what's next and have the tools to adapt seamlessly when the time comes. A word of caution: I know for me, I can get stuck in planning for contingencies. The key is to strike a balance—spend enough time to feel prepared, but not so much that it detracts from focusing on the main plan.

Innovative thinking is also a key component of a forward-thinking mindset and the creative engine behind adaptability. It allows us to approach challenges from new angles and perspectives, devise fresh solutions, and turn obstacles into opportunities. Instead of sticking to conventional methods, innovative thinkers explore new ideas, experiment with different solutions, and embrace out-of-the-box approaches.

Innovative thinking empowers individuals to drive change by challenging the status quo and exploring new ideas and solutions. It awakens our creativity and a willingness to take risks in order to solve problems in unique ways and discover opportunities others might overlook. By embracing this mindset, we can break through barriers, influence progress, and adapt to evolving situations with originality as change agents. Using out-of-the-box thinking, we can inspire and lead change and have greater and more meaningful impact on our worlds.

During your career, have you ever gotten training to better prepare for possible industry trends or to learn new technology?

As social media was evolving, I know many of my entrepreneurial friends with small businesses started taking courses and getting training on how to capitalize on this trending marketing tool. Their growth mindset, curiosity, strategic foresight, and innovative thinking positioned them to thrive in the new world online.

Flexibility, communication, continuous learning, and forward-thinking all contribute to adaptability by enabling individuals to adjust to change, work together in concert, grow through new experiences, and proactively prepare for future challenges. They are essential qualities that together form the foundation of adaptability.

Flexibility helps us stay open and adjust quickly when situations shift, while strong communication skills allow us to collaborate and build understanding with others during transitions. By embracing continuous learning, we actively seek out new skills and perspectives in order to effectively handle new challenges and trust our decisions. Using a forward-thinking mindset, we are able to plan ahead and think creatively, turning uncertainty into opportunities for growth. These qualities together enable us to adapt to change with resourcefulness and a clear sense of direction.

The Role of Emotional Intelligence

But adapting to change is more than just logistics—it's also about understanding and managing emotions.

Using your EQ to understand your emotions and what might trigger fear, frustration or other stress responses allows you to step back and harness your emotions. Rather than letting them control you, you are able to channel them to guide your actions towards positive change. Emotional intelligence also enables you to recognize, understand and positively influence the emotions of others to effectively navigate change.

Empathy and self-awareness are components of EQ that also contribute to adaptability.

As discussed in previous chapters, Empathy comes into play in all kinds of situations. Imagine helping a friend adjust to a big life change, like becoming a parent or moving to a new country. Being empathetic means understanding what they're feeling and offering support that meets their needs. It's not about fixing everything for them; it's about showing you care and helping them feel capable of handling the situation.

Self-Awareness is equally important. Let's say you're training for a marathon, but partway through, you realize your original pace is too ambitious. Recognizing this without beating yourself up and adjusting your approach to something sustainable is self-awareness in action. It's about being honest with yourself and making changes that keep you moving forward.

Emotional intelligence, empathy, and self-awareness are essential traits that strengthen adaptability by fostering both personal and interpersonal growth. Emotional intelligence helps individuals manage their own emotions while understanding and responding to the emotions of others, which is critical during times of change. Empathy deepens connections by allowing individuals to see situations from other perspectives, promoting collaboration and trust. Self-awareness enables individuals to recognize their strengths, limitations, and emotional responses, allowing them to approach challenges with clarity and adjust their actions as needed. Together, these qualities create a strong foundation for navigating uncertainty, building relationships, and adapting effectively to new circumstances.

Why Women Excel at Adaptability

Women have a unique ability to excel at adaptability, rooted in both natural strengths and lived experiences. Emotional intelligence and empathy, foundational traits for many women, enable us to understand diverse perspectives and respond thoughtfully to change. This relational approach fosters collaboration and helps guide others through uncertain situations. Our ability to adapt to multiple roles and manage complex challenges—whether balancing personal responsibilities or professional demands—further sharpens our ability to pivot and adjust as circumstances evolve.

The cultural and social conditioning many women face also plays a role in strengthening adaptability. Navigating systemic barriers and biases builds resilience, teaching us how to thrive despite obstacles. The dual roles women often juggle in personal and professional spheres enhance flexibility, equipping us with the tools to respond resourcefully to unpredictable situations. This constant balancing act refines our ability to find solutions that work, even when faced with competing priorities.

Whether leading during a crisis or fostering long-term change, we are able to embrace adaptability and navigate complexity to drive progress.

The challenges women face and overcome are often the very experiences that make us adaptable and resilient. Whether breaking through systemic barriers, balancing multiple roles, or responding to unexpected changes, we learn how to thrive in dynamic and uncertain environments. As women, we have long navigated significant challenges in a predominantly male-dominated world. These experiences often cultivate exceptional adaptability and resilience, equipping us to handle uncertainty, setbacks, and change with remarkable effectiveness as business leaders.

If you haven't yet, get your free downloadable companion Workbook at cathyholt.com/unstoppableworkbook to go deeper on the chapter, write down your thoughts, and consider these takeaways and action steps.

Key Takeaways

1. Adaptability is a Critical Leadership Trait

Adaptability is the ability to stay flexible, embrace change, and adjust effectively to new circumstances. It is a cornerstone of leadership, enabling women to navigate uncertainty, think creatively, and remain focused on long-term goals.

2. The Interplay Between Adaptability and Resilience

While adaptability allows leaders to pivot and respond to change, resilience provides the inner strength to persevere and recover from setbacks. Together, these traits create a cycle of growth and progress, empowering women to thrive in dynamic environments.

3. Women's Unique Strengths in Adaptability

Women's emotional intelligence, empathy, multitasking abilities, and collaborative problem-solving skills enhance their adaptability. These traits allow women to manage complex roles and respond resourcefully to shifting demands in both personal and professional spheres.

4. Why Adaptability Matters

Leaders who adapt to change with flexibility and creativity inspire confidence and foster innovation. Adaptability allows leaders to view challenges as opportunities, remain open to new ideas, and turn uncertainty into growth.

5. Components of Adaptability

- **Flexibility:** Adjust quickly to immediate changes without abandoning long-term goals.

- **Communication:** Foster trust and alignment through clear and transparent communication during transitions.

    ○ **Continuous Learning:** Stay open to acquiring new skills and knowledge to remain relevant and agile.

    ○ **Forward-Thinking Mindset:** Anticipate future challenges and opportunities with curiosity, creativity, and strategic foresight.

The Role of Emotional Intelligence

Emotional intelligence, including empathy and self-awareness, strengthens adaptability. These qualities allow leaders to manage emotions, understand others' perspectives, and foster collaboration during times of change.

Women's Adaptability in Action

Women's ability to juggle multiple responsibilities and navigate systemic challenges equips them to handle change and uncertainty with remarkable effectiveness. These experiences cultivate adaptability as a leadership superpower.

By fostering adaptability through continuous learning, emotional intelligence, and forward-thinking strategies, women can thrive as leaders, inspire others, and drive meaningful change in their communities and organizations.

Practical Steps to Cultivate Adaptability in Leadership

1. Embrace a Learning Mindset:

Actions such as committing to personal development, exploring training opportunities, and staying current in your industry demonstrate a proactive approach to learning. These practices show you are open to growth, willing to acquire new skills, and prepared to adapt to evolving circumstances.

2. Encourage Innovation and Experimentation:

Volunteering for new projects and suggesting process improvements reflect a willingness to embrace change and experiment with new ideas. These actions encourage creativity, foster innovation, and demonstrate your ability to think outside the box and adjust to new opportunities.

3. Manage Uncertainty Strategically

Determining what is in your control versus what is not helps manage uncertainty by focusing your energy where it can make a difference. Being responsive to new information, asking questions, and conducting research ensure you remain agile and informed, even when navigating unpredictable situations.

4. Champion Change Effectively:

Actions like taking on stretch goals, being open to new roles and responsibilities, and working collaboratively with diverse teams demonstrate a readiness to embrace change and adapt to shifting circumstances. These behaviors highlight your capacity to lead others through transitions with a forward-thinking and resilient mindset.

5. Demonstrate Initiative and Proactivity:

By suggesting improvements, joining new projects, or shadowing colleagues, you show that you are not only comfortable with change but also actively seeking opportunities to contribute and grow. This positions you as a leader who thrives in dynamic environments.

These practical steps create a strong foundation for adaptability and resilience by fostering openness to change, cultivating a growth-oriented perspective, and equipping you with the tools to navigate challenges with confidence and clarity.

Chapter 8

Resilience in Leadership

Resilience is the ability to recover from setbacks, adapt to change, and continue growing, even when faced with adversity. It combines strength, flexibility, and determination, enabling individuals to confront challenges, persevere, and thrive. Resilient people recognize that the journey is as important as the destination, using obstacles as opportunities to develop adaptability, sharpen problem-solving skills, and build confidence in their ability to overcome difficulties.

This dynamic process draws on both inherent strengths, such as determination and creativity, and learned skills gained through experience and coping strategies. Resilience is not an innate trait but a skill that can be nurtured and strengthened through intentional effort, supportive relationships, and access to resources. It involves maintaining balance and perspective during tough times while fostering emotional flexibility, cultivating a positive mindset, and making choices that prioritize personal well-being. Like any skill, resilience requires ongoing practice and a commitment to growth. empowering individuals to navigate life's challenges and create opportunities for a fulfilling future.

People who are resilient draw on both their inherent strengths, such as determination and creativity, and the skills they've learned through experience and coping with hardships. Resilience is something they develop over time through intentional effort, the support of others, and access to helpful resources. They maintain balance and perspective during tough times, practice emotional flexibility, cultivate a positive mindset, and make choices that prioritize their well-being. Like any skill, resilience requires ongoing effort and dedication. Through consistent practice and a commitment to growth, resilient people navigate life's challenges and create opportunities for a more fulfilling future.

This chapter will explore the concept of resilience, breaking down its key components and examining how it empowers individuals to overcome adversity, maintain balance, and thrive in the face of challenges. Through practical strategies and real-life examples, it will highlight how resilience can be cultivated as a critical skill for personal and professional growth.

Components of Resilience

The foundations of resilience are diverse and interconnected, encompassing emotional, cognitive, and behavioral elements that help individuals navigate challenges and thrive in adversity.

Emotional regulation, self-awareness, (they're back—both elements of emotional intelligence) and **optimism** create a strong emotional foundation for resilience. They help you maintain balance, understand your inner world, and approach challenges with a mindset that fosters growth and recovery. These two qualities keep surfacing as leadership skills because a self-aware leader can effectively handle complex situations, make better decisions, build stronger relationships, and empower others to grow and expand their impact.

Emotional regulation and self-awareness are deeply interconnected components of resilience. Self-awareness involves recognizing and understanding your emotions, thoughts, and behaviors, while emotional regulation is about managing those emotions effectively once they are identified. Together, these skills enable you to respond to challenges with intention and composure rather than reacting impulsively.

If you notice that you're feeling anxious about a difficult conversation—that's self-awareness. Rather than succumbing to the anxiety, you decide to take steps to calm yourself—like pausing to breathe, reframing your perspective, or planning what to say   so you can approach the situation constructively—that's emotional regulation.

When combined, self-awareness and emotional regulation empower you to maintain balance and a clear head even in high-pressure or stressful situations. They help you identify triggers and patterns in your emotional responses, enabling you to adapt and respond in ways that align with your goals and values. This combination fosters a sense of control and emotional stability, which are critical for navigating adversity and building resilience over time. Together, they form a foundation for thoughtful, adaptive decision-making in the face of life's challenges.

A heightened sense of self-awareness increases resilience. When you take the time to understand your strengths and where you can grow, it becomes easier to adjust, learn what you need, and make decisions that truly reflect who you are. Being in tune with your thoughts and emotions and knowing what can trigger negativity sharpens your ability to replace harmful or unproductive thought patterns with more supportive and encouraging ones.

Optimism is the ability to maintain a hopeful and positive outlook, even in difficult situations. It significantly enhances resilience by reducing feelings of helplessness that often occur when people feel they have no control. Having an optimistic outlook encourages you to take intentional steps to address and improve a situation rather than feeling stuck or giving up. It's about focusing on what can be done, even when the circumstances are difficult, and using that energy to find solutions, make progress, or manage the impact of the challenge. For example, instead of dwelling on a project setback, constructive action might involve brainstorming alternative solutions, seeking advice, or taking small steps toward a larger goal. Optimists are more likely to believe that difficulties can improve, encouraging persistence and adaptability. Additionally, optimism strengthens social connections by encouraging positive interactions and supportive relationships, which are essential for emotional support during tough times. This proactive approach helps build resilience by fostering a sense of control and purpose. Optimism also reduces the risk of becoming paralyzed by negative emotions, allowing you to move forward with confidence and hope.

Emotional regulation, self-awareness, and optimism form a solid emotional foundation for resilience, enabling you to stay balanced, understand yourself deeply, and face challenges with a mindset that encourages growth and recovery.

Cognitive Elements of Resilience

The cognitive elements of resilience are the mental processes and attitudes that enable individuals to navigate challenges, solve problems, and maintain a sense of control and purpose. These components shape how we interpret adversity, approach solutions, and adapt to change, forming a critical foundation for building and sustaining resilience.

Resilience is deeply rooted in the way we think, process challenges, and approach life with purpose. A growth mindset plays a key role, allowing us to see obstacles not as insurmountable barriers but as opportunities to learn and grow. This mindset fosters persistence, creativity, and an openness to improvement, helping us approach difficulties with curiosity rather than fear. Coupled with strong problem-solving skills, we can analyze situations critically, break down complex challenges into manageable steps, and find practical solutions that keep us moving forward.

Equally important is adaptability, the ability to remain flexible in our thoughts and perspectives when faced with change. As discussed in Chapter 7, adaptability and resilience are intertwined. People who adjust quickly to new circumstances, exploring alternative approaches and embracing uncertainty as a chance for growth, are both adaptable and resilient. Considering diverse perspectives and being able to adjust your thinking and decisions when you gain new information are signs of cognitive adaptability. This flexibility is strengthened by self-efficacy, the belief in our ability to influence outcomes and achieve goals. When we trust in our capabilities, we face challenges with confidence and take proactive steps to overcome obstacles.

Underlying all these elements is a deep sense of purpose and meaning, which provides direction and motivation, especially during tough times. A clear sense of purpose helps us put challenges into perspective and stay focused on what truly matters. Together, these cognitive elements work in harmony, enabling us to approach life's difficulties with determination, resourcefulness, and the ability to grow stronger through adversity.

Let's delve a bit more deeply into these qualities.

A growth mindset is the belief that abilities and intelligence can be developed through effort and learning, which is fundamental to resilience. It emphasizes viewing difficulties not as roadblocks but as valuable opportunities for development. This mindset helps us shift our focus away from fear of failure and encourages us to embrace challenges with determination and innovation. By prioritizing progress over perfection, a growth mindset enables us to remain driven and receptive to new ideas, ultimately strengthening our capacity to overcome obstacles and adapt to adversity.

Effective problem-solving is a cornerstone of resilience because it empowers individuals to face challenges with clarity and purpose. This ability goes beyond just finding answers; it involves assessing the situation from multiple perspectives, anticipating potential roadblocks, and crafting well-thought-out solutions to address them. People who are resilient approach problems methodically, breaking them into smaller parts, and devising incremental action steps to avoid feeling overwhelmed. They often rely on creative thinking and adaptability to uncover innovative solutions that might not be immediately obvious. This skill not only helps resolve current difficulties but also strengthens their capacity to tackle future challenges with greater ease and assurance. Over time, effective problem-solving becomes a cycle of learning and growth, enhancing resilience with each successfully navigated obstacle.

Imagine your business loses a major client, creating a significant revenue gap. Instead of panicking, you assess the financial impact, cut costs, and brainstorm new revenue streams, possibly marketing to potential clients and modifying or expanding your services. You strengthen relationships with existing clients who already know and like you. Throughout the process, you are adapting and adjusting your business strategies based on feedback and new opportunities that arise. By tackling the issue step by step and maintaining a forward-thinking mindset, you are more likely to not only recover from the setback but emerge with a more resilient business. Imagine how many businesses had to pivot during COVID-19 to survive, demonstrating the power of effective problem-solving and resilience.

Self-efficacy is the confidence in our ability to influence outcomes and accomplish our goals, even when faced with challenges. This belief fosters a sense of control over our circumstances, which is essential for building resilience. Individuals with strong self-efficacy trust their ability to solve problems, adapt to change, and persist through difficulties. They are more likely to think things through and act, make informed decisions, and stay motivated, even when there are obstacles or uncertainty in their path. This proactive approach helps them tackle challenges head-on, turning them into opportunities for growth. Self-efficacy not only strengthens resilience but also encourages a positive and empowered mindset, enabling individuals to recover more quickly from setbacks and maintain momentum toward their goals. This unwavering trust in their own capabilities is a key driver of resilience, providing both the confidence and determination needed to thrive in adversity.

A sense of purpose and meaning serves as a powerful anchor during life's challenges, providing both motivation and clarity, which are essential for resilience. When we understand your core values, passions, and the things that matter most to us, we develop a clear sense of direction that helps us stay focused and determined, even in the face of adversity. This clarity allows us to frame challenges not as insurmountable obstacles but as part of a larger journey that aligns with our deeper purpose, helping us maintain perspective and emotional balance.

Having a strong sense of purpose also fuels perseverance, giving us a reason to keep moving forward when circumstances feel overwhelming or uncertain. It acts as a guiding force, enabling us to prioritize what truly matters and make decisions that reflect our values and long-term vision. Resilient people draw deeply on this inner compass, finding strength not only to endure adversity but to adapt, grow, and emerge stronger. This connection to purpose sustains hope, enhances strategic decision-making, and builds the determination needed to turn setbacks into opportunities for progress and success.

Together, these cognitive components create a powerful framework for resilience, enabling individuals to approach life's challenges with a mindset that fosters learning, adaptability, and confidence.

Behavioral elements of resilience

Resilience is not built in isolation—it thrives through our interactions with others, the ways we manage our stress, and our ability to adjust our actions in response to change. These behavioral components of resilience are essential for navigating life's challenges, as they provide the tools and support needed to stay grounded, flexible, and proactive in the face of adversity.

A strong support network is the foundation of resilience, offering emotional, practical, and psychological resources to uplift individuals during challenging times.

Healthy relationships—whether with friends, family, colleagues, or mentors—serve as a safety net when challenges arise. A good support network doesn't just offer encouragement; it provides a space to share experiences, gain insights, and receive constructive feedback. For instance, talking through a problem with someone you trust can bring clarity to complex situations and help you see solutions you might not have considered on your own.

Support networks also foster a sense of belonging and connection, which is critical for emotional well-being. Knowing that others care about and believe in you can be a source of strength, especially when your confidence is shaken. Cultivating these relationships requires effort—showing empathy, maintaining communication, and being willing to ask for and offer help. A well-maintained support network is not just about leaning on others during hard times but also about building mutually beneficial relationships that enrich everyone involved.

Stress is an inevitable part of life, but how we manage it plays a significant role in building resilience. **Effective stress management** means actively using techniques that reduce tension, calm the mind, and help us regain control in difficult moments. Practices like mindfulness, for example, encourage individuals to stay present rather than getting caught up in worries about the future or regrets about the past. This presence can reduce the emotional intensity of stress and create space for thoughtful decision-making.

Physical activity is another powerful stress-relief tool. Exercise, whether it's a brisk walk, a workout, or yoga, helps release endorphins, which improve mood and energy levels. Even short bouts of physical activity can help clear the mind and provide a mental reset. In conjunction with exercise, it is also crucial to get enough sleep. As sleep success coach Johann Callaghan points out, sleep is essential to life and basic functioning, productivity, and performance. Poor sleep has a significant impact on our physical, mental, and emotional health and in turn a negative impact on our relationships, our ability to learn, our memories, our health and safety, and our quality of life. And, whether you go for a calming walk or smash a ball on the tennis court to relieve pent up energy, physical activity can relieve stress.

Relaxation techniques, such as deep breathing or progressive muscle relaxation, are equally valuable. They help regulate the body's stress response by slowing the heart rate and calming the nervous system. Journaling allows us to process their emotions, organize our thoughts, and gain clarity, helping to reduce tension and promote a sense of calm.

The key to stress management is consistency. Building daily habits that prioritize mental and physical well-being ensures that we have tools readily available when stress levels spike. By managing stress effectively, we create the capacity to approach challenges with a clear mind and calm demeanor, which are essential for resilience.

Allow me to take a moment to reflect on the concept of our circle of control as it relates to behavioral elements of resilience. One of my mentors, Julie Miller Davis, helped me truly understand this concept.

When we look at our lives, there is really just a small portion of it that is in our control. The list of aspects of our lives that we typically can control include our thoughts, actions, responses to situations, the choices we make, how we allocate our time, our attitude, the effort we invest in achieving our goals, the boundaries we set, the knowledge we pursue, and the ways we care for our physical and mental well-being. Taking responsibility for, and concentrating our energy and efforts on, those things we can control helps us develop an attitude that we can effect positive change. We are more apt to challenge those pesky negative thoughts that so often try to derail us. Successfully dealing with the things in your power to affect nurtures that growth mindset you've read so much about. It also fuels your mental wellness and sense of power over your life, while also developing your flexibility when confronting new circumstances.

In life, there is a larger "circle" that represents everything outside our control. This includes events, situations, and the actions or decisions of others. While some of these things may be influenced—like how we communicate with someone to affect their perspective or how we prepare for potential challenges—they ultimately remain outside our control.

When we focus on this outer circle, we end up worrying too much about the things we cannot control. This can lead to frustration, stress, and wasted effort. Recognizing the boundary between what's within our power and what isn't allows us to approach life with clarity and a sense of purpose, enabling us to adapt and thrive even when the uncontrollable feels overwhelming.

The circle of control is closely tied to mental toughness and resilience, as it helps leaders focus their energy on what they can influence rather than becoming consumed by external factors outside their control. By encouraging leaders to prioritize their actions and mindset, this concept not only reduces stress but also strengthens their ability to remain composed and effective in the face of adversity. It is a powerful tool for maintaining clarity and fostering a resilient approach to challenges.

Adaptability on a behavioral level means being willing and able to adjust your actions to meet the demands of changing circumstances. It's the practical application of flexibility: letting go of rigid plans and taking intentional steps to respond to new realities. This might involve shifting priorities, learning new skills, or even rethinking long-term goals in response to unforeseen challenges. For example, a person navigating a sudden career change might explore new industries, take online courses, or start networking to open up new opportunities.

Behavioral adaptability is not about abandoning plans but rather about modifying them to stay effective in the face of change. This requires both a willingness to take risks and the humility to accept when an approach isn't working. Adaptable individuals embrace the idea that progress doesn't always follow a straight line. They focus on what they can control—such as their actions and attitude—while remaining open to alternatives that may arise along the way.

This capacity to pivot not only ensures forward movement during uncertain times but also fosters a sense of agency and confidence. By consistently taking steps that align with the present reality, individuals strengthen their resilience, turning challenges into opportunities for growth and reinvention.

Together, these elements—strong support networks, effective stress management, and behavioral adaptability—form a comprehensive framework for resilience. They empower us to navigate life's challenges with clarity, composure, and confidence, ensuring we not only recover from adversity but also grow and thrive.

I imagine that by now you are sensing that all these qualities and skills are deeply interconnected, forming the foundation for effective leadership and personal growth.

The Intersection of Adaptability and Resilience

Adaptability and resilience are deeply interconnected, each reinforcing the other to create a powerful foundation for navigating challenges and thriving under pressure. When women are adaptable, they demonstrate the flexibility to adjust to new circumstances and embrace change, which in turn strengthens their resilience by reducing the emotional toll of uncertainty. Equally, resilience provides the mental fortitude to face adversity, enabling leaders to approach challenges with the confidence needed to adapt. Together, these qualities form a feedback loop that not only sustains us through difficult situations but also enhances our ability to grow and succeed.

I have had the privilege of getting to know Anne, the executive director of PolyCom Girls, through collaborations we've forged in our work at the UN. Anne's story begins in Kibera, the largest urban slum in Africa, where she grew up believing that hunger, threats of sexual violence, housing insecurity, devastating floods, and constant chaos were universal experiences.

Her perspective began to shift when she was granted the opportunity to attend boarding school as a teenager—an experience she recognizes as a privilege, despite the challenges it brought. Leaving her friends and family behind and adapting to new norms, spaces, and expectations was daunting, yet it exposed her to a different way of life. In high school, Anne slept in her own bed for the first time, and when she lacked a blanket, her classmates generously gave her one. She shared meals regularly and formed friendships that have lasted to this day.

Amidst these changes, Anne embraced a growth mindset. She believed that her hard work, abilities, and willingness to learn could pave a new path for her future. She persevered through her challenges, completing her secondary education, and credits those moments of discomfort and uncertainty as the times when she experienced the greatest growth.

During school vacations, Anne would return to Kibera, motivated to share her experiences with the girls in her community. She spoke of a world beyond their immediate surroundings—a world of opportunities for women and girls. Her leadership journey eventually brought her back to Kibera permanently, where she has dedicated herself to empowering and uplifting the next generation. As the executive director of PolyCom Girls, Anne works tirelessly to help girls in Kibera grow, flourish, and realize their potential, demonstrating through her life and leadership the transformative power of resilience and vision.

Adaptable leaders are often more resilient under pressure because they view change as an opportunity rather than a threat. For example, a leader managing a team during a sudden organizational shift might quickly assess the new circumstances, reallocate resources, and pivot strategies to meet the demands of the moment. Their adaptability keeps the team moving forward, while their resilience ensures they stay focused and composed, even in the face of setbacks. This combination of skills inspires confidence in their team, fostering trust and collaboration during challenging times.

Resilience, in turn, fosters the confidence to embrace adaptability. A resilient leader, grounded in their ability to recover and learn from setbacks, is more likely to take calculated risks and experiment with new approaches. This willingness to adapt not only solves immediate problems but also creates opportunities for growth and innovation. For example, when faced with a failed project, a resilient leader might analyze what went wrong, extract valuable lessons, and use those insights to develop a more effective strategy. Over time, this adaptive mindset strengthens their resilience, creating a virtuous cycle of growth and capability.

Greta Thunberg, the Swedish climate activist, is a powerful example of adaptability and resilience. Living with Asperger's syndrome, which she describes as her "superpower," Greta uses her unique perspective to maintain sharp focus and unwavering commitment to her mission of combating climate change. Her ability to embrace her differences and channel them into strengths underscores her resilience and determination.

What began as solo school strikes in Sweden at the age of 15 rapidly evolved into a global movement, requiring Greta to adapt to new and complex challenges. She mastered the art of addressing world leaders, delivering speeches at international forums, and inspiring millions across cultures and generations. The attacks against Greta Thunberg have largely sidestepped climate science, focusing instead on discrediting her personally, as well as targeting her family and motives. These assaults have included doctored sexualized images and threats of violence. Her critics have attempted to undermine Greta by questioning her mental health, labeling her as "deeply disturbed," "unstable," or "mentally ill." Despite the hostility, Greta continues to face such attacks with remarkable resilience, maintaining her focus on climate advocacy and refusing to be silenced by intimidation.

Greta's journey demonstrates an extraordinary ability to turn obstacles into opportunities for growth and advocacy. Her resilience is evident in how she navigates the pressures of public life while staying grounded in her principles. Her adaptability shines as she shifts from grassroots activism to global diplomacy, all while maintaining authenticity and a clear sense of purpose.

Through her example, Greta reminds us of the transformative power of adaptability and resilience in leadership. She shows that with focus, determination, and a deep connection to purpose, it is possible to overcome challenges, inspire change, and leave a lasting impact on the world.

Adaptive and resilient leaders have a far-reaching impact that goes beyond their personal achievements. By modeling flexibility and strength, these leaders motivate teams to think creatively and pursue innovation, collaborate effectively, and approach complex challenges with confidence. They cultivate a culture that embraces change, prioritizes continuous learning, and fosters collective resilience, allowing individuals and teams to thrive. Through their ability to integrate adaptability and resilience, these leaders not only address immediate challenges but also lay the groundwork for sustainable growth and success in an ever-evolving landscape.

Why Women Excel at Resilience

Women's resilience is not simply a product of innate traits but a reflection of their ability to leverage emotional intelligence, navigate societal challenges, and adapt to complex, ever-changing roles. These qualities, combined with their determination and resourcefulness, enable women to rise above adversity, lead with strength, and inspire those around them.

As we addressed in previous chapters, emotional intelligence and empathy are foundational traits that contribute significantly to women's adaptability and resilience. These qualities enable women to connect deeply with others, understand diverse perspectives, and foster collaboration in ways that drive effective leadership. Emotional intelligence helps women navigate complex interpersonal dynamics, while empathy allows them to build trust and create environments where people feel valued and supported.

Women's aptitude for managing multiple roles and complex challenges not only enhances their adaptability but also strengthens their resilience, positioning them as highly effective leaders. Whether balancing careers with caregiving responsibilities, community leadership, or societal expectations alongside personal ambitions, women constantly navigate dual roles that require flexibility, time management, and emotional strength. This constant juggling sharpens their ability to stay organized, think creatively, and pivot under pressure. These experiences build both adaptability and resilience, enabling women to adjust to changing circumstances, recover from setbacks, and approach challenges with determination. As a result, women excel in leadership roles that demand innovative solutions, composure, and the ability to thrive in uncertain and dynamic environments.

Navigating systemic barriers and biases has significantly shaped women's resilience. Challenges such as unequal access to opportunities, gender stereotypes, and glass ceilings have taught women to persevere, adapt, and remain resourceful. These experiences often cultivate grit, determination, and emotional strength—core aspects of resilience. Women frequently face higher expectations and limited resources, whether battling gender biases or managing unequal workloads in professional and domestic spheres. These obstacles compel them to think creatively, develop innovative solutions, and find ways to succeed despite the odds.

For many women leaders, overcoming these difficulties has involved challenging traditional norms, advocating for themselves in male-dominated spaces, and building strong support networks to advance their careers. These efforts not only reinforce resilience but also foster a sense of empowerment that fuels their leadership. Women's natural strengths, combined with the resilience honed through navigating systemic barriers and societal expectations, uniquely position them to excel in adaptability and resilience. By leveraging these qualities, women leaders can overcome challenges and inspire and empower others to do the same.

Women prioritize building and maintaining strong social connections, which provide emotional and practical support during tough times. These networks not only offer a source of encouragement but also create a foundation for shared learning and collective problem-solving, enhancing resilience.

If you haven't yet, get your free downloadable companion Workbook at cathyholt.com/unstoppableworkbook to go deeper on the chapter, write down your thoughts, and consider these takeaways and action steps.

Key Takeaways

1. **Resilience as a Dynamic Skill:**

    a. Resilience is the ability to recover from setbacks, adapt to change, and grow through adversity.

    b. It is not innate but can be cultivated through intentional effort, supportive relationships, and access to resources.

2. **Emotional Foundations of Resilience:**

    a. Self-awareness and emotional regulation are critical for managing emotions and maintaining composure in high-pressure situations.

    b. Optimism fosters persistence and adaptability, encouraging action and reducing feelings of helplessness during challenges.

3. Cognitive Components of Resilience:

a. A growth mindset allows individuals to view challenges as opportunities for development.

b. Problem-solving skills and adaptability enable leaders to analyze obstacles, craft solutions, and adjust their approach as circumstances evolve.

c. A strong sense of purpose provides motivation and clarity, helping individuals navigate adversity with direction and focus.

4. Behavioral Elements of Resilience:

a. Building and maintaining support networks fosters emotional and practical resources during tough times.

b. Effective stress management techniques, such as mindfulness, physical activity, and prioritizing self-care, help maintain balance and clarity.

c. Behavioral adaptability ensures forward momentum by encouraging intentional adjustments in response to change.

5. The Intersection of Adaptability and Resilience:

a. Adaptability and resilience reinforce one another, creating a cycle of growth and capability.

b. Leaders who integrate these qualities inspire confidence, motivate teams, and foster cultures of innovation and collaboration.

6. Women's Strengths in Resilience:

a. Women excel at resilience due to their emotional intelligence, ability to manage complex roles, and capacity to navigate systemic challenges.

b. Their experiences balancing careers, caregiving, and societal expectations hone adaptability and resourcefulness.

c. Strong social connections and a sense of purpose empower women to thrive and lead with strength.

7. Leadership Impact:

a. Resilient leaders inspire teams, model flexibility and strength, and create environments where individuals and organizations can thrive.

b. By integrating resilience and adaptability, leaders build a foundation for sustainable growth and success in dynamic, ever-changing environments.

Practical Steps for Building Resilience for Women

1. Cultivate Self-Awareness

o Reflect on emotions, strengths, and areas for growth through journaling or mindfulness.

o Recognize energy-draining triggers and address them proactively.

2. Strengthen Resilience

Stress Management and Self-Care Practices:

- o Focus on what is within your control to reduce stress and foster emotional balance.

- o Prioritize self-care through mindfulness, physical activity, and mental clarity during challenging times.

Developing a Support Network:

- o Build strong relationships by volunteering for new projects or working with diverse teams, which provides opportunities to form meaningful connections.

- o Lean on support networks for guidance and encouragement, strengthening your ability to navigate tough situations.

Cultivating Optimism and Persistence:

- o Set stretch goals with supervisors or colleagues, even if they feel challenging, to build persistence and demonstrate growth through effort.

- o Embrace change in projects or processes to reinforce a positive and adaptable mindset.

3. Focus on What You Can Control

- o Identify actionable areas and let go of worries about factors beyond your influence.

- o Break challenges into manageable steps to maintain clarity and confidence.

4. Embrace a Growth Mindset

o   Reframe challenges as opportunities to learn and improve.

o   Celebrate progress, even small achievements, and use setbacks as lessons to refine your approach.

5. Strengthen Adaptability

o   Stay open to new skills, ideas, and experiences.

o   Volunteer for challenging roles or projects that expose you to diverse perspectives and opportunities.

6. Foster Optimism and Positivity

o   Focus on solutions rather than problems and surround yourself with uplifting influences.

o   Practice gratitude and acknowledge the positives in your life, even during adversity.

7. Find and Nurture Your Sense of Purpose

o   Identify what drives and motivates you, such as your career, family, or a cause you care about.

o   Align your actions with your core values to create a sense of direction and strength.

8. Commit to Continuous Learning

o   Pursue personal and professional growth through training, workshops, or mentoring.

    o   Stay informed about industry trends and treat every experience as an opportunity to grow.

9. Advocate for Yourself

    o   Speak up about your needs, boundaries, and goals in personal and professional settings.

    o   Celebrate your achievements and recognize your worth, reinforcing your confidence.

Resilience is a cornerstone of effective leadership and personal growth. It empowers individuals to face challenges with strength, flexibility, and determination while fostering adaptability and innovation. By cultivating resilience, leaders not only overcome adversity but also inspire and empower others, leaving a lasting impact in their organizations and communities.

Chapter 9

Personal Growth and Growth Mindset for Leadership for Women

At this point in the book, I think that it is apparent how many of these qualities and skills are integral to awakening our leadership capabilities. These traits interconnect because leadership is not a set of isolated skills but a dynamic, holistic practice where each trait reinforces and enhances the others.

But why should you prioritize personal growth and development? Because it enhances self-awareness, strengthens relationships, builds confidence, and increases adaptability... all traits essential for effective leadership. By fostering personal growth, leaders can advance their careers, inspire others, and create a more fulfilling and balanced life. It also equips you with resilience and a positive mindset to navigate challenges while cultivating a deeper sense of purpose and satisfaction in your personal and professional journey.

As discussed in earlier chapters, personal growth is a continuous journey of learning, self-reflection, and embracing challenges as opportunities for development. It involves understanding your strengths and areas for growth, adapting to change, and striving for progress in all aspects of life. A growth mindset is central to this journey, empowering individuals to view effort, practice, and persistence as keys to unlocking potential. By focusing on personal growth, you build the resilience and confidence needed to navigate life's complexities with purpose and fulfillment. This mindset emphasizes lifelong learning—not just acquiring skills but embracing setbacks as opportunities to evolve and strengthen your ability to adapt with creativity and determination.

For women in leadership, personal growth and a growth mindset are particularly critical for overcoming societal and structural barriers, such as gender bias, underrepresentation, and limited access to resources. These challenges can be formidable, but a commitment to self-improvement equips women with the resilience, adaptability, and confidence needed to thrive in demanding roles. Embracing these traits not only enables personal success but also positions women as role models who inspire and mentor others, creating a ripple effect of empowerment and positive change.

Leadership for women is deeply influenced by the interplay of identities such as race, gender, sexuality, ability, and socioeconomic background—a concept known as intersectionality. These overlapping identities shape leadership experiences in profound ways, presenting unique challenges like navigating stereotypes, microaggressions, systemic biases, and exclusion. By understanding and embracing intersectionality, women leaders can approach their distinct paths with greater self-awareness and use their diverse experiences to foster equity and inclusion in the spaces they lead.

The intention of this chapter is to provide you with a deeper understanding of how personal growth and a growth mindset are critical for developing and sustaining effective leadership, especially for women navigating diverse and intersecting identities. It will explore how cultivating self-awareness, embracing challenges, and reframing failures as opportunities can empower leaders to continuously evolve, while also addressing the unique dynamics of intersectionality—how race, gender, sexuality, ability, and other identities shape leadership journeys. By examining the connection between personal growth, a growth mindset, and intersectionality, you should gain actionable strategies to develop resilience, adaptability, and a commitment to lifelong learning. You should also learn how embracing these elements helps leaders overcome self-doubt, navigate systemic barriers, and lead with confidence, authenticity, and inclusivity in their personal and professional spheres.

Personal Growth: The Foundation for Leadership

Personal growth is a transformative journey of self-discovery and improvement that equips you with the knowledge and skills to unlock your potential and achieve meaningful goals. It encompasses self-awareness, adaptability, and emotional intelligence—qualities that form the foundation for authentic and effective leadership. For women, personal growth often intersects with the need to challenge societal expectations, overcome self-limiting beliefs like imposter syndrome, and navigate spaces where they are underestimated or excluded.

At its core, personal growth requires a commitment to self-reflection and learning. We must cultivate self-awareness to understand our motivations, values, and blind spots, enabling us to lead with clarity and purpose (Chapter 2). Skill development, including both technical expertise and interpersonal skills, prepares us to handle the complexities of modern challenges, such as managing change, addressing competing demands, and solving intricate problems with creativity and collaboration. Emotional intelligence further enhances leadership by fostering trust, effective communication, and the ability to manage emotions constructively (Chapter 3).

For women, growth often involves recognizing and addressing systemic barriers, such as biases or role congruity—the prejudice that arises when a person's social identity, like gender, is perceived as mismatched with leadership qualities. These barriers are not personal failings but reflections of societal inequities. For instance, being labeled "too aggressive" when asserting yourself may stem from biases about how women "should" behave, rather than the merit of your actions.

Turning these obstacles into opportunities for growth means leveraging personal experiences to advocate for change while fostering collaboration. Women supported by allies and organizations committed to diversity, equity, and inclusion (DEI) can spotlight inequities and push for policies that foster fairness—not just for themselves but for others. This shared responsibility creates environments where marginalized voices are valued, ensuring that barriers are dismantled rather than endured.

In these moments, women are not just overcoming adversity— they are leading transformative change. By co-creating opportunities for progress, they drive systemic change while fostering cultures of equity and inclusion. This collective approach ensures that growth is not an isolated burden but a shared journey toward a more equitable future.

By prioritizing personal growth, women can create leadership styles rooted in authenticity and resilience, inspiring others to grow and thrive in their own journeys.

Defining Growth Mindset

A growth mindset is the belief that abilities, intelligence, and talents can be developed through dedication, effort, and learning. This contrasts with a fixed mindset, where individuals view their capabilities as innate and unchangeable. Remember my daughter coming home from school and saying she wasn't good at math because it wasn't in her DNA—that's a fixed mindset. My daughter training and competing for a chance at the Olympics in her equestrian discipline of three-day-eventing was an example of a growth mindset. Her belief in herself and her hard work and dedication led her to participate in the equivalent of the equestrian "Junior Olympics" before she had her stroke.

A person with a fixed mindset often avoids challenges, has a fear of failure, and resists feedback, because they feel their abilities are inherent and unalterable. In contrast, someone with a growth mindset confronts challenges head on, trusting that they are capable of learning whatever is needed to succeed. They view new or difficult tasks as opportunities to improve. Those with a growth mindset see setbacks as a delay in their pursuit rather than failure, and consider them as stepping stones to achieving their goals rather than a reflection of their worth or capability. People with a growth mindset are often more resilient and accomplished both in their personal and professional lives.

A growth mindset empowers aspiring leaders and those in leadership roles to approach their personal and professional journeys with curiosity and resilience. It encourages them to prioritize learning and view setbacks as opportunities to reassess, adapt, and improve rather than as reflections of their abilities. This mindset fosters confidence in facing uncertainty, helping individuals stay resourceful and focused even in challenging situations. For women and underrepresented leaders, a growth mindset can be particularly transformative, enabling them to overcome self-doubt, challenge stereotypes, and build a strong sense of capability as they pursue their goals with purpose and authenticity.

The Science of Growth Mindset

Research in psychology and neuroscience has shown the transformative power of a growth mindset. These studies show that the brain is malleable, capable throughout life of forming new connections—a concept known as neuroplasticity. This means individuals can strengthen abilities and develop new skills with consistent effort and practice. When my daughter was learning how to walk again after her stroke, her brain was forming new connections around the injured part of her brain. If you've ever learned a different language, your brain has actually gone through structural changes. You create more gray matter in the area of the brain that processes language and increase neural connections.

Research by Carol S. Dweck, a Stanford University professor whose research has defined the field of mindset psychology, highlights how mindset influences motivation, perseverance, and overall success. For example, those with a growth mindset tend to persist longer and perform better after setbacks compared to those with a fixed mindset. And they are more likely to learn from their mistakes.

How Mindset Shapes Behavior and Achievement

A growth mindset profoundly shapes behavior by fostering curiosity, encouraging individuals to embrace challenges, and promoting a willingness to seek and act on feedback. Those with this mindset approach new situations with an open mind, seeing them as opportunities to learn and grow rather than as threats. This openness leads to greater confidence in taking risks and experimenting with innovative solutions, as they view setbacks not as failures but as valuable learning experiences.

For leaders, a growth mindset extends beyond personal behavior—it creates a ripple effect. Leaders who embody adaptability and continuous learning serve as role models, inspiring those around them to adopt similar attitudes. They cultivate spaces where exploration and improvement are valued, encouraging others to take initiative and share ideas. This fosters trust and supports the development of more dynamic, resilient, and forward-thinking organizations.

In personal and professional contexts, a growth mindset helps you build stronger relationships, navigate uncertainty without getting overwhelmed or reactive, and remain focused on long-term goals despite obstacles. This mindset not only shapes how you act but also influences how others perceive and respond to you or your leadership.

Cultivating a growth mindset requires intentional effort, self-reflection, and the ability to embrace challenges.

Practical steps include:

- **Reframing Challenges**: View difficulties as opportunities to learn rather than threats to avoid. For example, instead of fearing failure, focus on the lessons that setbacks provide.

- **Embracing Feedback**: Feedback, even when critical, is a valuable tool for improvement. A growth mindset sees constructive criticism as a gift, not a judgment.

- **Learning from Failure**: Mistakes are inevitable, but they are also some of the most effective teachers. Cultivating a growth mindset involves recognizing the value in failure and using it to grow stronger and more capable.

The Role of Reflection, Journaling, and Cultural Humility:

- **Reflection**: Regular self-assessment helps identify areas for improvement and celebrate progress. Leaders can ask themselves, "What did I learn today?" or "How can I approach this differently next time?"

- **Journaling**: Writing about challenges and successes reinforces learning and provides a record of personal growth. It also helps process emotions and clarify thoughts.

- **Cultural Humility**: Recognizing that growth is not just an individual journey but also a relational one. Cultural humility involves acknowledging biases, valuing diverse perspectives, and continuously seeking to understand and learn from others' experiences.

By actively cultivating a growth mindset, individuals can unlock their potential, overcome systemic barriers, and contribute to more inclusive and innovative leadership environments.

Success is not rooted in a single career tip or productivity hack. It's shaped by your outlook and attitude. The ability to shift from a negative mindset to a positive one, from a fixed mindset to a growth mindset, and from a scarcity mindset to an abundance mindset is transformative. This mental shift sets the stage for overcoming obstacles and unlocking your full potential, bringing you closer to your goals with each step forward.

As is true for all women to advance their leadership journey, each step into the unknown holds the potential for transformation. Stay open to change—it can be the gateway to new possibilities and a more fulfilling career journey.

Intersectionality, Leadership, and a Growth Mindset

Intersectionality and a growth mindset are deeply interconnected, as both emphasize embracing complexity and using it as a foundation for growth and empowerment. The term "intersectionality" was coined by legal scholar Kimberlé Crenshaw to describe how overlapping aspects of identity—such as race, gender, sexual identity, ability, and socioeconomic background—create unique experiences of privilege and discrimination.

For women leaders, particularly those who experience marginalization due to their intersecting identities, a growth mindset becomes an invaluable tool for navigating compounded challenges. A growth mindset encourages individuals to view obstacles as opportunities to learn and grow rather than as insurmountable barriers. For women navigating systemic inequities shaped by intersectionality, this mindset fosters resilience and adaptability, enabling them to persist through biases, stereotypes, and exclusion with creativity and determination. It empowers them to thrive in environments often not designed to accommodate their diverse experiences, turning adversity into a catalyst for leadership growth.

Understanding intersectionality also enhances a leader's growth mindset by fostering deeper self-awareness and empathy. Crenshaw's insights encourage leaders to reflect on how their identities influence their own journeys while recognizing the diversity of challenges faced by others. This awareness not only strengthens their personal growth, but also drives them to create more inclusive and equitable spaces. By integrating the principles of intersectionality into their growth mindset, women leaders empower themselves while advocating for systemic change, ensuring that these spaces become more accessible and representative for all.

Leadership journeys are deeply shaped by the complexity of intersectionality. This framework is vital for understanding how these interconnected identities influence access to opportunities, perceptions of authority, and barriers faced in professional spaces. It recognizes that the challenges people face and their experiences in life are shaped by the interplay and layering of these factors, rather than by a single identity alone.

For women marginalized by race, disability, socioeconomic status, or other intersecting identities, the leadership journey is often shaped by navigating environments not designed to accommodate their experiences. These overlapping factors create compounding challenges, such as unequal access to resources, heightened scrutiny of their abilities, and relentless pressure to prove their worth. As they progress in their leadership roles, these women must draw on personal resilience to succeed within these constraints while also working to challenge and transform the systems that perpetuate inequities.

For women with marginalized identities, intersectionality creates unique barriers that profoundly impact their leadership journeys. These challenges often force them to balance personal growth with a broader commitment to equity and inclusion. However, their resilience and adaptability allow them not only to overcome these obstacles but to lead with strength and purpose, using their experiences to inspire systemic change and create more inclusive leadership spaces. For example:

- **A woman of color** may have to navigate exclusion from decision-making spaces due to gender, while also facing racial biases that question her authority.

- **A woman with a disability** might deal with accessibility issues and stereotypes about her abilities, which can undervalue her potential to lead.

- **A woman from a low-income background** may lack traditional educational opportunities, forcing her to forge unconventional paths that reflect creativity and resilience.

These personal experiences often require marginalized women to innovate and adapt as they carve out leadership roles, challenging structures that were not designed for them. The weight of navigating such challenges isn't just personal—it reverberates outward, reshaping leadership for others who face similar barriers.

Take the story of a grassroots leader from Peru; I call her Rosaria. Her leadership journey began with uniting women in her community to create local soup kitchens. This project grew into a movement supporting over a quarter-million people through 4500 soup kitchens across 55 regions of Peru. The established patriarchy initially felt threatened by Rosaria's community organizing. She was often harassed and denied access to resources. Eventually, when local authorities recognized the benefits of her work, collaborations were established. Similarly, when Rosaria began attending global meetings to share her grassroots organizing strategies, she was dismissed because of her "simple" and diminutive demeanor, her minimal formal education, and limited ability to speak English. Rosaria's persistence and growth mindset, coupled with support from grassroots women's networks like the Huairou Commission, helped elevate her to global leadership. Today, she advocates for grassroots women worldwide, proving that individual leadership grounded in lived experiences can spark widespread change.

When women with intersecting marginalized identities step into leadership roles, they challenge stereotypes and redefine who belongs in positions of power. They often navigate stereotypes that undermine their authority, microaggressions that chip away at their confidence in a macro way, and systemic biases that limit access to advancement opportunities. For instance, a leader who is both LGBTQ+ and a person with a disability may face dual forms of discrimination that amplify the challenges of being accepted and recognized in leadership roles.

For those with privilege, the leadership journey often includes fewer obstacles, as systems are structured to accommodate aspects of their identity, such as race, gender, socioeconomic status, education, or ability. Privilege refers to unearned advantages, like access to higher education or being able-bodied, which can open doors and provide resources, mentorship, and networks that facilitate advancement. Recognizing privilege isn't about guilt—it's about awareness. By understanding how these systems favor certain groups, individuals can use their privilege responsibly to help create more equitable opportunities for others.

The interplay of personal experiences and broader impact showcases how marginalized women's leadership journeys are not just about overcoming challenges but about reshaping the spaces they lead, inspiring systemic change, and empowering others to follow their example. Their success sends a clear message: leadership rooted in authenticity, resilience, and lived experience is transformative—not just for individuals, but for the systems and communities they touch.

Social narratives about marginalized identities often perpetuate fixed mindsets by reinforcing self-limiting beliefs. For example, stereotypes such as "women aren't natural leaders," "disability is a limitation," or "success is unattainable without wealth" can discourage women from pursuing opportunities or embracing challenges. These narratives can create fear of failure or feelings of not belonging, which hinder personal and professional growth.

A growth mindset, however, challenges these limiting beliefs. Women marginalized by race, disability, or socioeconomic background can reframe these external narratives by focusing on their ability to learn, grow, and contribute meaningfully. For example:

- A woman with a disability might reframe accessibility issues as opportunities to advocate for systemic change, making her voice heard and benefiting others in similar situations.

- A woman from a low-income background might view her unconventional path as a source of creativity and innovation, bringing fresh perspectives to leadership.

- Women facing tokenism can shift their focus from external validation to self-empowerment, recognizing their unique value and contributions.

By embracing a growth mindset, these women not only navigate challenges but also redefine their leadership journey in ways that reflect their authenticity and resilience.

Intersectionality and Leadership: The Experiences of BIPOC Women

I want to preface this section with the acknowledgement of not being a woman of color. What I present here is based on my being the mother of a Brazilian American daughter with disabilities, having been married for 25 years to a Brazilian man while immersing myself in the Latin culture, living in Brazil for 5 years, and working globally with grassroots women in many situations where I was the only white woman at the table and where I had to develop trust as an ally. Additionally, I work as a consultant in the diversity, equity, and inclusion space, which has demanded continuous learning and cultural humility.

For BIPOC (Black, Indigenous, and People of Color) women, the leadership journey is shaped by the complex interplay of race, gender, sexual identity, and often additional factors such as socioeconomic background or ability. These intersections create unique challenges, including compounded barriers like racial biases, gender stereotypes, microaggressions, tokenism, and systemic inequities. For example, a Latina leader may face the double bind of navigating expectations to conform to traditional gender roles while also confronting racial assumptions that undermine her authority. These overlapping forms of discrimination amplify the difficulty of advancing in professional spaces, requiring BIPOC women to exhibit heightened resilience and adaptability.

Representation plays a critical role in shaping the leadership journeys of BIPOC women. In industries and organizations where leadership remains predominantly white and male, the lack of role models with shared lived experiences can make the path to leadership feel isolating and uncertain. As Marian Wright Edelman, civil rights activist and founder of the Children's Defense Fund, reminds us, "You can't be what you can't see." Yet representation must go beyond mere visibility—it involves creating opportunities, amplifying voices, and ensuring that leadership reflects the diversity of the communities it serves.

Many BIPOC women in leadership positions take on the dual responsibility of excelling in their roles while paving the way for others. They work to dismantle barriers, foster equity, and create environments where diverse talent can thrive. Despite systemic challenges, their lived experiences often become a source of strength. Cultural awareness, empathy, and the ability to bridge diverse perspectives enrich their leadership and enable them to advocate for inclusion and systemic change.

At the same time, the weight of deeply entrenched obstacles— microaggressions, biases, and the expectation to represent an entire community—can be exhausting and frustrating. Changing leadership paradigms should be a shared responsibility, and addressing inequities cannot fall solely on the shoulders of BIPOC women. Creating inclusive spaces requires systemic effort and allyship at every level.

The connection between a growth mindset and the experiences of BIPOC women in leadership is nuanced and impactful. A growth mindset—the belief that abilities and intelligence can be developed through effort, learning, and persistence—offers significant value to BIPOC women as they navigate systemic barriers and overlapping challenges shaped by intersectionality

By combining representation, resilience, and a commitment to equity, BIPOC women are redefining leadership to reflect the strength and diversity of their communities. Their contributions show that inclusive leadership benefits not only individuals but entire organizations and societies, offering a transformative vision of what leadership can and should be.

Redefining Leadership Models Through Intersectionality and Growth Mindset

Traditional leadership models often reflect narrow ideas of success, rooted in privilege, hierarchy, and individualism and historically defined by white men. These approaches can leave out the richness of diverse voices and experiences. Redefining leadership through an intersectional lens and a growth mindset means opening the door to more inclusive and varied ways of leading.

For many women, leadership is less about individual accomplishments and more about shared progress. They often focus on community, collaboration, and collective success— approaches that reflect a growth mindset by prioritizing long-term impact over short-term gains. These models create leadership that uplifts others, fosters mutual support, and drives meaningful change for everyone involved. By redefining leadership, we make space for all voices, ensuring that diverse contributions are valued and that leadership reflects the communities it serves.

Authenticity, Community, and Growth Mindset in Leadership

For women dealing with layered identities that can create biases about their capabilities, being true to themselves can be one of their greatest strengths as leaders. Owning and embracing their full identities allows them to approach leadership with honesty and confidence, drawing power from the unique experiences that have shaped them. Executive leadership coach Farah Hussain advises clients who are women of color that "Your authenticity is a unique contribution you can make to your environment." Knowing who you are comes from reflection and self-discovery—a key activity of the growth mindset. This authenticity helps view challenges as chances to learn and grow.

Having a supportive community is also key to keeping that growth mindset alive. Whether it's through mentorship, support groups, or professional networks, connecting with others who've faced similar experiences can be incredibly validating. Creating a network of allies who offer encouragement, shared wisdom, and a sense of solidarity helps women stay resilient and amplify their voices. For me, an ally is someone who actively supports you both personally and in public. Hussain also recommends that we should all "identify potential allies in the spaces where we experience the greatest challenge of being seen, heard, or understood."

We all have layers of identity. Some of those identities provide us with advantages and disadvantages in any given situation. With the support of a strong community, our leadership journey becomes a shared effort, rooted in collaboration and mutual strength.

What is Personal Growth and Why Is It Important for Aspiring Leaders?

Personal growth is the ongoing process of self-improvement, development, and learning that helps us reach our full potential. It involves cultivating self-awareness, expanding skills, and enhancing emotional intelligence to better navigate personal and professional challenges. (Does all this sound familiar?) At its core, personal growth is about embracing change, seeking continuous learning, and striving to become a more capable and fulfilled version of ourselves. And it's not always easy. Changing our habits, mindset, and choices requires dedication and determination. It means not staying stuck in the past, but knowing ourselves, our strengths and foibles, and going after what we truly want in life.

But for aspiring leaders, personal growth is crucial because it lays the foundation for effective leadership that genuinely reflects who you are. Leadership is not just about managing tasks or guiding others—it's deeply tied to your values and goals. By investing in personal growth, aspiring leaders develop the resilience to handle setbacks, the adaptability to navigate complex situations, and the self-awareness to understand their strengths and areas for improvement. Are you seeing how interconnected these traits are and how they are all integral to being the best you?

Furthermore, personal growth equips leaders with the ability to connect with others on a meaningful level. Emotional intelligence—a key component of personal growth—helps leaders empathize with diverse perspectives, communicate effectively, and build trust. Aspiring leaders who prioritize personal growth are better prepared to inspire and motivate others, foster inclusive environments, and approach challenges with creativity and confidence. Ultimately, personal growth is not just a tool for leadership success but a lifelong journey that enriches every aspect of your life.

It's time to get comfortable with discomfort! Growth thrives on change and challenges. Setting stretch goals—those ambitions that feel just beyond your current capabilities—forces you to develop new skills, perspectives, and resilience. These goals demand that you push past your existing limits, embrace uncertainty, and trust in your capacity to grow over time. Stretch goals aren't about immediate success; they're about transformation and stepping into a higher version of yourself.

However, it's important to approach these goals with a mindset of patience and persistence. Growth is rarely linear, and setbacks are an inherent part of the journey.

As the famous female comedian Carol Burnett said, "We all get where we're going by circuitous journeys, and some of the setbacks are warranted."

Every failure or obstacle presents an opportunity to learn, adapt, and refine your approach. The path to achieving stretch goals will likely include moments of doubt, frustration, and recalibration—but these experiences are where the most valuable lessons lie.

Resilience becomes the cornerstone of progress. The willingness to embrace roadblocks and persist despite them separates those who grow from those who stagnate. By setting ambitious goals and understanding that the journey is as important as the destination, you cultivate adaptability, problem-solving skills, and an unshakable belief in your ability to overcome challenges.

Ultimately, the process of pursuing stretch goals is as rewarding as achieving them. It transforms how you see yourself and the world, helping you discover untapped potential and opening doors to opportunities that once seemed out of reach. With every step forward, whether it's a leap or a stumble, you inch closer to realizing the full breadth of your capabilities.

Lifelong Learning and Skill Acquisition for Women

Lifelong learning is particularly transformative for women, as it empowers them to navigate unique challenges, break through barriers, and lead with confidence in spaces where they may be underrepresented. We must intentionally commit to continuously expand our knowledge, learn new skills, and adapt in a rapidly changing world. Leadership today demands more than traditional expertise; it requires a willingness to embrace newness in technologies, strategies, and perspectives in our personal and professional lives.

- **Leveraging Online Courses, Workshops, and Coaching**: Women can benefit from targeted learning opportunities that address leadership and skill development in contexts that resonate with their experiences. Online platforms and workshops tailored for women in leadership, such as negotiation skills, public speaking, or work-life integration strategies, can provide valuable insights and practical tools. Coaching is another powerful resource, offering personalized guidance to help women set goals, overcome challenges, and amplify their strengths.

- **Tailoring Skill Development to Specific Identity-Based Needs**: Women often face unique challenges, such as gender bias or societal expectations, that may shape the skills they need to thrive. For example, women of color might focus on advocacy skills to navigate and challenge inequities in their workplaces. I think all women can benefit from skills like building allyship, negotiating confidently, or managing implicit bias. Such skills are particularly valuable for women seeking to lead authentically while fostering inclusivity and equity.

By embracing lifelong learning and cultivating habits that align with our unique experiences and aspirations, we, as women can build the skills, confidence, and resilience needed to thrive. These practices empower us to lead authentically, overcome barriers, and inspire others on their journey of growth.

Creating Habits for Continuous Growth for Women

For women, especially those balancing multiple roles in their personal and professional lives, creating sustainable habits for growth is vital. By establishing daily practices and measures of accountability, we are more likely to grow. These habits allow us to prioritize our development while managing the demands of leadership and daily life.

- **Daily Routines for Reflection and Mindfulness**:
  We can all benefit from carving out time for reflection to review our values and goals, celebrate our progress, and identify areas for improvement. Journaling about daily experiences or practicing mindfulness techniques, such as meditation or gratitude exercises, can enhance emotional well-being and build resilience. These practices are particularly important in helping us manage stress and maintain focus amid competing priorities.

- **Strategies to Maintain Motivation and Accountability**:
  The best way for us to sustain motivation is by surrounding ourselves with supportive networks, such as women's professional groups or mentorship circles, where we can share experiences, exchange advice, and celebrate wins. I have my posse (that's Texan for group) that I can consult when trying to set realistic, actionable goals. They give me a reality check, to make sure my stretch goal isn't me trying to conquer the moon, and keep in touch about my progress. I have also relied on

accountability partners and coaches (sometimes formally and informally) who can provide encouragement and constructive feedback so I stay committed to my personal and professional growth.

Facing challenges and setbacks is an inevitable part of growth, but how you respond to them defines your resilience and shapes your success.

Dealing with Setbacks and Criticism

I want you to banish the word failure from your vocabulary. When we don't succeed at something, it is just an opportunity to learn why and try it again. As President John F. Kennedy said, "An error does not become a mistake until you refuse to correct it."

Criticism is part of life. One of my favorite coasters says, "Stop trying to make everyone happy, you're not tequila." But learning to handle setbacks with confidence can turn them into stepping stones. Seeing setbacks as temporary and focusing on what you can learn from them helps you bounce back stronger. Feedback, even when it's hard to hear, can be a chance to sharpen your skills and grow if you approach it with a growth mindset.

Balancing Growth with Life's Demands

Balancing personal growth with the demands of work, family, and everything else can be tricky, but it's doable with some planning. Managing your time and preserving your energy are key—set clear priorities and don't be afraid to say no when you need to. Taking care of yourself, whether that's through rest, reflection, or doing something you love, helps you stay on track without burning out.

Building Resilience and Emotional Intelligence

Once again, we are seeing these valuable traits in action. Resilience and emotional intelligence are superpowers that can help you stay steady and connect with others. Managing stress with simple habits like mindfulness or taking breaks keeps you focused when things get tough. Building stronger relationships by improving communication and showing empathy—especially with people from different backgrounds—makes life and leadership a lot smoother.

If you haven't yet, get your free downloadable companion Workbook at cathyholt.com/unstoppableworkbook to go deeper on the chapter, write down your thoughts, and consider these takeaways and action steps.

Key Takeaways

1. Personal Growth and Leadership are Interconnected:

a. Personal growth is a continuous journey that enhances self-awareness, resilience, and adaptability—qualities essential for authentic and effective leadership.

b. Leadership is shaped by the unique identities and experiences that influence how we navigate challenges and engage with the world.

2. The Power of a Growth Mindset:

a. A growth mindset enables women to view obstacles as opportunities for learning and growth, fostering resilience and flexibility.

b. By embracing a mindset of curiosity and persistence, women can overcome barriers, challenge stereotypes, and lead with confidence and creativity.

3. Authenticity is Key to Leadership:

a. The best leadership comes from staying true to ourselves and leading with a sense of purpose. Authenticity allows leaders to connect meaningfully with others and inspire trust.

b. Embracing our experiences and values strengthens our leadership style, making it more impactful and empowering.

4. Diversity in Leadership Matters:

a. Everyone's leadership journey is unique, shaped by the identities and experiences that make them who they are.

b. These differences demonstrate that there is no one "right" way to lead and that diverse perspectives and approaches enrich leadership, creating inclusive and dynamic environments.

5. The Ripple Effect of Personal Growth:

a. Personal growth not only strengthens individual leaders but also creates pathways for others to rise. By investing in their development, women leaders pave the way for more inclusive and equitable leadership spaces.

6. Practical Strategies for Growth:

a. Reframe challenges as opportunities to learn and grow, using setbacks as stepping stones to success.

b. Cultivate habits such as self-reflection, mindfulness, and skill-building to stay focused and resilient.

c. Build a network of support and seek out mentors, allies, and communities that uplift and inspire growth.

Practical Steps for Enhancing Personal Growth

1. Reflect on Your Identity and Strengths:

Take time to explore how your unique experiences and identities shape your leadership style and perspective. Tools like journaling or discussions with trusted mentors or peers can help you recognize your strengths and identify areas for growth.

2. Set Meaningful Personal Growth Goals:

Define clear, actionable goals that align with your values and aspirations. Whether it's improving a skill, addressing self-doubt, or expanding your network, focus on steps that support your long-term leadership journey.

3. Embrace Lifelong Learning:

Continuously seek opportunities to expand your knowledge and skills through online courses, workshops, or coaching. Prioritize resources that address both universal leadership principles and challenges unique to your identity and experiences.

4. Build a Strong Support Network:

Surround yourself with other women leaders and allies who share your commitment to growth. Engage in communities where you feel valued, can collaborate, and find inspiration through shared experiences.

5. Prioritize Self-Care and Resilience:

Incorporate habits that promote well-being, such as mindfulness, exercise, or reflection. These practices help you stay grounded, manage stress, and maintain focus, allowing you to approach challenges with adaptability and strength.

6. Commit to Continuous Growth and Adaptability:

Leadership isn't about achieving perfection—it's about making consistent progress. Embrace change as an opportunity for growth, own your unique journey, and remain committed to evolving into the leader and changemaker you aspire to be. Every step forward brings you closer to achieving your potential and leaving a meaningful impact.

Final Thought:

Leadership thrives on the combination of personal growth, authenticity, and diverse perspectives. By embracing their journeys and adopting a growth mindset, women can lead with strength, purpose, and inclusivity, creating meaningful impact for themselves and others.

Chapter 10

Passion to Action

If you don't know this already, let me tell you—you have what it takes to be a leader. Maybe you are not strong in all these qualities, but I assure you, they are within you. Part of the leadership journey is discovering your inner strengths, developing them, and learning to use them strategically.

But why embark on this journey? Why put yourself out there to lead change? It's scary; sometimes you'll face criticism and even spark ire. What's in it for you?

When you step into leadership, you gain opportunities for personal growth, empowerment, and fulfillment. Leading allows you to amplify your voice, advocate for causes you care about, and create meaningful impact in your personal and professional lives, communities or organizations. It builds confidence, strengthens your networks, and enhances your ability to navigate challenges with resilience and adaptability. Leadership also provides a platform to inspire and mentor others, leaving a legacy of positive change. For many women, stepping into leadership is not just about professional advancement but also about embracing their unique strengths and realizing their full potential.

Embarking on a leadership journey is often sparked by a woman's passion to create meaningful change. Whether fueled by a desire to solve problems, uplift others, or challenge the status quo, this passion becomes the driving force for action. Recognizing the traits you already possess—qualities like empathy, emotional intelligence, resilience, adaptability, creativity, and visionary thinking—is the crucial first step. These strengths, often demonstrated in daily life through balancing family responsibilities, navigating career challenges, or fostering community connections, are more than everyday skills—they are the foundation of impactful leadership.

The journey begins when you align your values and vision with your goals, using these unique traits to chart a purposeful path forward. It's about turning passion into purpose, and purpose into plans, while embracing growth and overcoming self-doubt along the way. As you take bold steps, you transform your innate strengths into intentional strategies, inspiring others to collaborate, contribute, and build something greater than themselves. Through this process, you not only create ripples of meaningful impact, but also pave the way for others to follow, demonstrating that leadership is about acting authentically and leaving a legacy of positive change.

This process helps you on a personal level by fostering self-discovery, growth, and empowerment. As you embark on your leadership journey, you will gain a deeper understanding of your values, strengths, and purpose, which builds confidence and clarity in your decisions. Turning your passion into action enables you to feel a sense of fulfillment and alignment with your goals, creating a life of greater meaning and authenticity. By overcoming self-doubt and embracing growth, you not only unlock your potential, but also develop resilience and adaptability, essential for navigating challenges.

Through this journey, I experienced the joy of inspiring and uplifting others. My sense of purpose strengthened my relationships as I connected with my purpose and those I supported and who supported me along the way. Having the courage to step up and speak out reinforced my belief in my ability to lead as I set out to create a lasting impact on my community and beyond.

Embarking on this journey should transform your life as you replace those limiting beliefs with a growth mindset, embrace your power, and live a life that reflects your true potential, all while contributing to a legacy of positive change that benefits all you encounter.

I designed the L.E.A.D.S. framework because I wanted to create a leadership model that reflects the unique journey, strengths, and potential of women. Too often, leadership models are one-size-fits-all, overlooking the nuanced challenges women face and the distinctive qualities they bring to the table. L.E.A.D.S. is built to empower women to lead authentically, starting with self-discovery and building toward meaningful impact. It acknowledges the importance of empathy, EQ, adaptability, and resilience while also encouraging boldness, vision, and strategic action. My goal was to craft a framework that not only inspires women to step into leadership but also equips them with the tools and mindset to thrive. L.E.A.D.S. is a roadmap for personal and professional growth, designed to celebrate women's contributions and amplify their voices as leaders shaping a brighter, more equitable future.

I want to thank Wendy Barr of Intelligent Brands for challenging and guiding me in solidifying my leadership development experiences and knowledge into an actionable framework to share with women who want to lead the change they want to see.

The L.E.A.D.S Framework

L - Learn About Yourself: Engage in self-discovery to uncover your values, passions, and purpose. Understanding your authentic self forms the foundation for meaningful and impactful leadership.

E - Elevate Your Perspective: Broaden your understanding and seek diverse viewpoints. Activate your Empathy and Emotional IQ to maximize your leadership

A - Amplify Your Potential: Embrace opportunities for growth by refining your abilities, listening to feedback, and finding your authentic voice. Build confidence and lead boldly.

D - Design the Future: Take the lead in crafting a vision to drive change. Align your actions with your values to inspire progress and create a legacy of meaningful impact.

S - Strategize for Impact: Strategically apply your leadership skills to influence, inspire, and drive meaningful change. Use your strengths intentionally to leave a lasting legacy.

L.E.A.D.S. Framework in Action for Women Leaders: What Does It Mean?

Throughout this book I have identified and discussed different traits and skills that align with these five components of leadership development. In this list, I have grouped different skills as they apply to the action steps in the framework.

L - Learn About Yourself. Discover your unique strengths, passions, and purpose. Knowing who you are is the foundation for authentic leadership.

Self-reflection is a powerful tool in this process, helping you uncover the values and passions that drive your decisions and actions. By taking the time to look inward, you gain clarity about what truly matters to you and where your strengths lie. This deepened self-awareness not only builds confidence but also creates a strong foundation for authentic leadership. Through self-reflection, you can better understand the experiences that have shaped you, identify patterns in how you respond to challenges, and uncover opportunities for growth. Additionally, self-reflection allows you to let go of what no longer serves you by identifying beliefs, behaviors, and obligations that weigh you down and no longer align with your values. True personal growth isn't about adding more to prove your worth, but about shedding what holds you back, creating space for what truly matters. By releasing these unnecessary burdens, you can focus on what brings fulfillment, clarity, and joy, enabling you to live and lead with purpose, alignment, and integrity.

Problem-Solving: Turning Challenges into Opportunities
As natural problem-solvers, whether you're juggling work, family, or community commitments, you've probably faced challenges that required creativity and quick thinking. By reflecting on how you've tackled problems in the past, you'll uncover your core values and strengths. Engaging in self-discovery is a powerful act of personal growth and self-care, allowing you to recognize how each challenge has contributed to your leadership journey. Through self-reflection, you can enhance your problem-solving skills by identifying patterns in your decision-making, understanding which strategies were effective, and learning from past missteps. It refines your ability to evaluate situations with clarity, adapt swiftly, and develop innovative solutions, equipping you to face future challenges with confidence, resilience, and creativity. This heightened awareness empowers you to trust your instincts and lead authentically, even in the face of complexity.

E- Elevate Your Perspective is about expanding your understanding by embracing diverse viewpoints, stepping outside your comfort zone, and challenging assumptions. It encourages leaders to be curious about new ideas and open to learning from experiences that differ from their own. By seeking out diverse perspectives, you not only gain fresh insights but also develop the ability to approach challenges with a broader, more inclusive mindset. This process strengthens your leadership by fostering adaptability and creative problem-solving.

Rather than focusing solely on connection or communication, this step emphasizes the importance of cultivating a growth mindset—seeing every interaction, challenge, and perspective as an opportunity to learn and grow. It also highlights the leader's responsibility to create an environment where differences are valued, innovation is encouraged, and everyone feels empowered to contribute. By elevating your perspective, you become better equipped to make decisions that are both equitable and forward-thinking, inspiring those around you to embrace collaboration and change.

Communication: Inspiring Connection
Great leaders know how to connect with others, and women excel at this because we listen actively and adapt our approach. Whether you're giving feedback at work or talking with a friend, your ability to communicate with empathy fosters trust and engagement. By staying curious and open to feedback, you strengthen your growth mindset and improve how you inspire and connect with others.

Empathy: The Heart of Leadership
Empathy allows you to step into someone else's shoes and understand their emotions and perspectives. It's not just a "soft skill"—it's a powerful tool for creating trust and building meaningful relationships. By practicing empathy, you not only deepen connections with others but also develop emotional intelligence, a key part of personal growth that makes you a stronger leader.

Collaboration: The Power of Working Together
Women naturally value teamwork and inclusion, making us exceptional collaborators. By creating a space where diverse voices are heard, you foster innovation and build stronger, more connected teams. Collaboration is also an opportunity for personal growth—you learn from others, expand your perspective, and inspire a shared vision for success.

A - Amplify Your Potential. Say yes to opportunities that challenge you. Commit to lifelong learning, embrace a growth mindset, and step into your leadership with confidence and courage.

Amplifying your potential is about proactively seeking opportunities that help you grow, evolve, and lead with greater impact. This involves a commitment to lifelong learning, where you continuously build your skills, expand your perspective, and embrace new ideas. For women, who often face societal pressures and internal doubts (i.e. imposter syndrome), this step provides the tools to overcome barriers and step into leadership roles with confidence. But it's not just about reacting to change, but intentionally stepping into experiences that stretch your abilities and challenge your thinking. By approaching each opportunity with a growth mindset, you shift your focus from fearing failure to seeing every step as a chance to learn and improve.

This process also involves building confidence through action. The more you engage with challenging opportunities, the more you realize your own strength and capability. Amplifying your potential isn't about perfection—it's about progress and the courage to try. By leaning into growth and staying open to feedback, you unlock your capacity to lead authentically, while inspiring others to see and embrace their own potential. Through intentional effort and a mindset of continuous learning, you become not just a leader but a catalyst for change and growth.

Adaptability: Thriving Amid Change

Life loves to test our flexibility, and women are often at the forefront of adapting to change—whether it's managing career transitions, family dynamics, or unexpected challenges. Every time you pivot and grow, you build resilience and expand your capacity as a leader. Embracing change with a growth mindset helps you see it not as a setback but as an opportunity to learn, improve, and thrive.

Courage: Leading with Boldness

Courage isn't about being fearless; it's about taking action in the face of fear. Whether you're speaking up in a meeting, taking a personal or professional risk, or pursuing a dream, every bold step you take builds confidence and inspires others. Courage also fuels personal growth, because stepping outside your comfort zone is where real transformation happens.

Resilience: Rising Strong

Resilience is the ability to bounce back stronger after life's challenges. Women develop resilience through the ups and downs of balancing multiple roles and navigating cultural norms and systemic barriers. By reframing hardships as opportunities for growth, you embrace a mindset that sees challenges as stepping stones. Resilience is not just about surviving—it's about growing stronger and leading with renewed purpose.

D - Design the Future - Dream Big: Turning Vision into Reality

Dreaming big is about envisioning a future aligned with your values, passions, and purpose. It's also about identifying and taking action. For women, it often means pushing past societal expectations or self-doubt to pursue meaningful goals—whether leading a team, starting a business, or driving community change. A bold vision lays the foundation for impactful leadership, but it requires aligning your actions with your core values to stay focused and grounded.

Bringing your vision to life demands a growth mindset. Instead of viewing obstacles as roadblocks, see them as opportunities to learn, adapt, and grow. This mindset fuels resilience, creativity, and the courage to take risks, reminding you that progress is built through effort and persistence. It's about creating and implementing action steps to impact change.

As you move toward your goals, celebrate small wins along the way. Each step forward builds confidence and reinforces your belief in what's possible. By dreaming big, acting with purpose, and embracing a growth mindset, you create meaningful change for yourself and inspire others to believe in their potential to lead and make a difference.

Creative and Visionary Thinking: Seeing Beyond the Horizon

Visionary leaders imagine what could be and take action to make it real. Women are skilled at combining creativity with practicality, finding innovative ways to improve lives and inspire others. Whether you're launching a new project, driving social change, or mentoring others, visionary thinking allows you to connect today's actions with tomorrow's opportunities. A growth mindset helps you see obstacles as part of the journey, giving you the courage to keep moving toward your goals.

S - Strategize for Impact: Focus Your Energy for Meaningful Change. Strategizing for impact means using your actions with precision and intention to drive the changes you want to see. It's about focusing your energy on what truly matters, rather than trying to take on everything. Women often feel the pull to take on everything, but impactful leadership comes from knowing how to focus your energy on what truly matters and aligns with your core values and goals. It's not about spreading yourself thin—it's about identifying the issues you care about most and strategically channeling your skills, time, and resources to create meaningful results.

Start by clarifying the specific changes you want to make. By narrowing your focus, you can avoid being distracted by competing priorities. Align your efforts with your vision to stay focused on actions that produce high-impact goals.

Leverage your strengths and delegate or collaborate with others where needed. Direct your energy to areas where you bring the most value while empowering others to contribute. This ensures your efforts are efficient and effective, avoiding burnout while empowering others to join and lead.

Prioritize actions that create a ripple effect—initiatives that don't just solve today's problems but set the stage for lasting progress. Think critically about how your efforts today can lead to sustainable progress tomorrow while addressing the root causes of the challenge. By focusing your energy strategically, you maximize your leadership's impact, aligning your actions with your goals to create meaningful, measurable change.

Delegation: Empowering Through Trust

Delegation is more than just dividing tasks—it's about building trust and empowering others to shine. Women excel at recognizing people's strengths and helping them grow into their potential. Effective delegation creates opportunities for others to step up and succeed while freeing you to focus on the bigger picture. This intentional act demonstrates a growth mindset by encouraging learning and development in others while strategically applying your strengths to maximize impact.

Conflict Resolution: Turning Differences into Strengths

Conflict is inevitable, but it doesn't have to divide. Women often approach conflict with emotional intelligence, finding common ground and fostering mutual understanding. By turning disagreements into opportunities for collaboration, you strengthen relationships and build stronger teams. A growth mindset helps you see conflict as a chance to learn, adapt, and create better solutions for everyone involved.

Every part of the L.E.A.D.S. framework is built on personal growth and a growth mindset. These are the driving forces that help you evolve as a leader. Personal growth allows you to discover who you are and where you want to go, while a growth mindset helps you see every challenge and opportunity as a chance to learn and improve. Together, they empower you to lead authentically, inspire others, and leave a lasting legacy of meaningful change.

Call to Action

Your leadership journey is about stepping into your potential and making a meaningful impact. Whether you're aspiring to lead change but feel uncertain about where to begin or are looking to advance your leadership capabilities, now is the time to take action. Leadership is not about having all the answers—it's about embracing growth, aligning your actions with your values, and moving forward with purpose. You have the power to inspire and create the change you want to see. Start small, dream big, and take bold steps to elevate your leadership and impact. Step into your potential and power.

How I Can Support You

I'm here to support you no matter where you are on your leadership journey. If you're aspiring to lead change but aren't sure how to start, I'll help you identify your passions, uncover your strengths, and turn your ideas into actionable plans. If you're ready to take your leadership to the next level, I'll work with you to refine your skills, expand your influence, align your goals with your vision for change, and show you how to use your leadership strategically for maximum impact.

Together, we'll build the confidence and strategies you need to amplify your leadership potential and make a lasting impact. Through personalized coaching, mentorship, and practical tools, I'll guide you as you navigate challenges, embrace opportunities, and grow into the leader you are meant to be. Let's unlock your potential and create the meaningful change you aspire to achieve—together.

You have what it takes to be the next great changemaker. Your unique strengths, vision, and courage are exactly what the world needs right now. My mission is to ignite a movement of women leaders—bold changemakers—who are ready to use their talents to transform their lives, families, communities, and the world. I truly believe that women, with their empathy, resilience, and determination, are the key to driving the positive change our world needs most. Together, we can create a future shaped by women who lead with purpose, inspire with action, and leave a legacy of lasting impact. The time to lead is now—your time to shine is now.

About the Author

Cathy Holt is an internationally renowned speaker, a bestselling author, and a lifelong advocate for women's rights. Her book, *Unstoppable Women: Owning Our Voices, Leading Change*, is dedicated to empowering women as leaders and change-makers, and was featured to celebrities at the 2025 Oscars. She is also the joyful mother of a gifted daughter leader.

Cathy has spent over 35 years advancing gender equality through university courses in Women and Gender Studies, and political, policy, and advocacy work, including collaborations with the United Nations and global NGOs. As the co-founder of DEI Consultants, she brings the gender lens to championing Diversity, Equity, and Inclusion (DEI) practices to foster belonging and drive transformative change.

Cathy's work in DEI extends beyond the professional sphere. In 2003, she became the primary support for her 18-year-old daughter after a devastating stroke. Drawing on her DEI expertise, Cathy advocated for more inclusive and equitable accommodations for people with disabilities, transforming personal challenges into powerful opportunities for systemic change. This personal journey has strengthened her unwavering resolve to dismantle inequities and create spaces where everyone, regardless of their race, gender, socioeconomic status, or other personal characteristics has equal access to opportunities, rights, and treatment.

She also founded Catherine Holt Consulting through which she has mentored women worldwide—from grassroots activists to aspiring leaders—to recognize their innate strengths, amplify their voices, and lead with authenticity and impact by guiding them through trainings and workshops based on her proprietary framework, L.E.A.D.S:

L - Learn About Yourself
E - Elevate Your Perspective
A - Amplify Your Potential
D - Design the Future
S - Strategize for Impact

Learn more and connect with Cathy:

Contact: cathy@cathyholt.com
Website: CathyHolt.com
LinkedIn: www.linkedin.com/in/catherine-holt-hts
Facebook: www.facebook.com/catherine.holt.56/
Instagram: https://www.instagram.com/cathyhts/

Thank You!

Thank you so much for reading *Unstoppable Women.* I hope this book has impacted you and inspired you to own your voice and start leading change in your life and community.

If you enjoyed this book, would you share your honest review on the Amazon book page